POP ON THE BED

My Caring Memoirs

i

LOVE AS ALWAYS TO

Vin my husband

My Children, Jenny, Paul and Helen their partners
Joe Heidi and Duane

My Grandchildren Harry, Olivia, Elliot, Charlie,
Sophia and Ruby.

My step Grandchildren William, Ben and Jade.

DEDICATION

To carers young and old in communities, homes and hospitals thank you for your commitment and hard work.

To the carers I met on my journey, nurses, doctors and administration staff you were my mentors.

Contents

HELLO MY NAME IS MOIRA

I cannot believe I'm doing this, writing a book, but why not. People say everyone has a story to tell and write about what you know. What I do know is that I have, like many others, worked very hard in the NHS and this book has sort of been in my head for years. This story of my work and life while employed by the NHS in nine job roles and over thirty years of service, at ten hospitals. I mention people, events and places of work where I had no concerns, because my colleagues were altruistic, amazing and wonderful, frontline carers. Some recollections of nameless colleagues were not so selfless.

My favourite hospital was North Manchester General (NMGH) because it was familiar, I spent a lot of time there with hard-working grafters, my colleagues. I call NMGH the mother ship and you will find it on Delauneys Road in Crumpsall, North of Manchester, England.

Recently I read books written by staff who worked in the NHS, Adam Kay a comedy writer wrote "This Is Going to Hurt and Twas the Nightshift Before Christmas" from his diaries of being a junior doctor. John England wrote "NHS Dirty Secrets" a b o u t

1

bullying, cover-ups, discrimination, favoritism and whistleblowing. Peter Duffy wrote "Whistle in The Wind, covering life, death, detriment and dismissal (A whistle-blowers story). I was sort of relieved as well as shocked that I wasn't alone in my thoughts, what they wrote, in one way or another were my experiences too. I witnessed bullying, discrimination, favoritism and dismissal.

This book for me skims the surface of these issues, not because I don't want to write about them, this book is about caring at home and in hospitals, making ends meet and conversations I heard while at work.

The mother ship site was a large hospital with multiple abandoned rooms offices and buildings. Urban explorers entered the old decaying buildings where you see documents and detritus left as we abandoned room after room, building after building boarding up the past, far too expensive to demolish was the official line. Some of the abandoned buildings were eventually used for storage. Things are changing and my mother ship is being rebuilt.

The cellars in the main hospital were by far the warmest place in the building and at one point I believe a few homeless people sheltered there at night. The water pipes and cables ran the length of the building, asbestos cladding with warning stickers could be seen as you walked along the stone floor. The area was frequented by porters, smokers and administration staff collecting notes from individual rooms and small annexes that ran off the main cellar. Eventually these areas became off limits, however some colleagues still had to enter the area for their work.

The corridors on the first and second floor had bits of flooring missing with lumps and bumps under the covering that seemed to be glued down regularly rather than replaced, the smell of the glue really got into your nose. I remember the doors on some areas were heavy, you had to put your shoulder behind them to enter a room. The results of a ceiling collapse from pigeon excrement exposed the state of the building where staff attended training. Everyone recognised the state of the hospital and complained, it didn't seem to matter we accepted our lot.

The mother ship had its own rhythm, a beating heart, a strong sturdy workforce that knew how to challenge, we weren't easy. We may have challenged and complained but we were worth it, grafters definitely, trouble certainly, carers mainly and I loved the heart of that place and the people that worked within those walls.

If you remember me, you may be saying to yourself "who does she think she is writing a book?" You may also be wondering if I acknowledge you in these pages. Who knows, I may have absolutely loved the way you worked or the wonderful thing you did that stayed with me enough for me to write about it?

If I remember you? Thanks! For giving me some amazing, strange and occasionally scary memories. The wonderful humour and banter I'm recalling still makes me smile. I loved sharing our stories in groups, on evenings out and in quiet corners of the ward. Eating toast in the doctors' mess with the teams, our break from the early ward round, stimulating and occasionally outrageous conversations.

I'm writing my thoughts and recalled conversations, snippets, and scraps of memory, mainly in a job role order, a varied cluster of my reminiscing. I don't know if it will ever get published because I keep coming back to type some more, to change a line or two and add another snippet that came to mind.

I suppose I wish some of the accounts were never events, that never happened to me and I wonder if I will add those accounts to these pages.

My life in the hospital is mainly as anecdotes and snippets of memory now, realisations and reflections of my experience. Flashes of memory and conversations have brought a rush of emotion, a little anxiety, recalling feelings experienced while working in the NHS. I occasionally cry as I type, recalling those moments, and there were many. Like most memories the physical effects hit me in exactly the same way all these years later, I still feel the ache in my heart.

To the hundreds of people, I met on my working journey, I have no doubt only a handful of you will remember being part of it, but I may remember you. Patients indelibly etched in memory because of suffering or situation. Nurses that helped me settle into the strange world of working on a ward or clinic. Doctors and nurses with real character. Staff I met on corridors every morning who never failed to say hello. Even remembering those that couldn't look me in the eye one day and then were all friendly the next. Those that gestured with a nod as they passed, others with big beaming smiles and those with urgency in their eyes, hurrying along.

I remember amazing staff, real grafters, fantastic strong personalities and a few good managers. There were many with huge egos, some lazy buggers, quite a few bad managers, and those that worked the system. All working in a hospital with multiple wards and departments trying to comprehend and utilise the myriad of systems. Yes, there were many systems with numerous passwords to remember, each clinical room, toilet, IT system and department had individual passwords and codes.

Another favourite memory is recalling the feeling of adrenaline surging through me when an urgent or important situation emerged. Watching the teams work through a difficult challenge with logic and wisdom was fantastic, our team became stronger. I loved that feeling so organised, so dedicated such strong team work, we always pulled together. Amazing people, with one thing in common, earning a living while hoping to make a difference to patients.

Thinking how colleagues saw me was a bit of a challenge. Most will probably never see me again and the very small number I see are good friends and would probably use a nice description.

I'm going to be honest with myself, some will describe me as strong, sharp, angry and a little mouthy. Others will say I'm generous, caring and supportive, someone with a good work ethic "loud" will cry others, honest, challenging, competitive and a bit of a witch possibly the final cry. If you don't really know me you probably only saw a couple of my many faces. My husband would say, "you've got a face on today", and would tone myself down a bit. Occasionally, at work I would sparingly smile at a situation, but inside I would be annoyed or upset because I couldn't for whatever reason say or do what I instinctively wanted too, in that moment.

Most people working in the NHS want to provide good quality health care and plan for future generations. However, you always get one with a different agenda, it's how you manage them and that is often where hospitals and the NHS fail. Some managers don't know how to manage and live-in fear of losing their job, they stay under the radar, in denial of situations and issues around them.

At the start of my journey a nursing role was a desirable career and the position was held in great esteem. Over the years I witnessed many ward closures and a reduction in the number of nurses seen around the hospital. The desirable roles changed and supervision, management and weird initiatives became more attractive. Senior nurse left to join the huge number of target focused clip board huggers that walked the corridors. The number of administration roles increased and their pay overtook the nurses at management level. At one point I was a clip board hugger too.

I began working for the NHS in 1986 as a Nursing Auxiliary on a male surgical ward and a gynaecology clinic, you could say I started at the bottom. In 2018 I retired as a Quality Improvement Lead. Blundering my way through work and life, I encountered special and noteworthy moments, months littered with utterly drab routine unremarkable days, moments of wonderful laughter then traumatic events would be thrown in for good measure, days I would dread.

To describe these moments, I began collecting one-line reminders many years ago, gathering thoughts for this book, I only needed a couple of words to recall a moment that seems to be etched in my memory. My first role was on a nightingale ward off the main corridor, on the top floor of the hospital. Walking into the building on that first day holding my letter of appointment I can recall the smell, the atmosphere, the chipped paint and the continuous sound of trolley wheels and staff walking up and down the ward with the occasional alarm going off. The sound of water from taps and tea being poured. The visual environment on a ward is dull so your hearing becomes more astute.

When you first enter a hospital either as a patient or a member of staff, everything, sounds, feels and tastes different, all a little strange. Bland food, harsh thin washed-out bedding fabric and gowns, noises you cannot identify others that you shouldn't be able to hear, all rather too close. On entering wards in the early days, the first thing you noticed would be a smell, a very strange strong disinfectant mixed with all types of human smells. I don't know what happened to that disinfectant, they don't use it anymore, it was probably toxic.

All grades of nurses I met were busy, some ate on the go, others got a decent break, time to eat in the canteen. Most nurses worked longer than contracted and my memory of working on wards in a nursing capacity were of hard- working team players who supported each other. I also remember lots of laughter and giggling through shifts. I believe nurses today work longer hours, have fewer breaks and there is in general less laughter, less joy in the work. I used to get concerned about staffing levels at the beginning of my career, nurses would voice surviving a shift without a disaster. Now hospitals are declared unsafe because they need more nurses, yet they stay open. Have we abandoned all thoughts of safe staffing in the NHS? I believe retiring staff are grateful they got through the job without making any significant errors. They survived. Most, like me will miss the camaraderie, patients and families.

At one point in 2019 I believe there were 40,000 nurse vacancies and one in twenty training places not filled. That's a shocking state of affairs for the NHS. I believe nursing is a vocation, a sort of life mission. Despite everything, the nurses turn up, and they did, through snow, wind and hail. I remember witnessing that mostly at Fairfield General Hospital in Bury when the snow was deep and the cars got stuck the nurses put on their wellies and walked, they may have been late but they always arrived. Nowadays expectations differ and if your life work is a vocation, you are definitely exploited and took advantage of.

I also believe in a life and work life balance which the NHS finds very difficult to offer its staff, competing with businesses that offer so much more from free parking, flexible working and weekends off, bonuses, on site general practice health care for all staff, regular hours; child care the list goes on. How will the NHS compete if it continues with managers in denial that don't provide flexible rotas, lots of job sharing and perks. It's not rocket science.

This book of my memories isn't meant to be funny, cathartic or anything else. It won't be grammatically

9

correct either. It doesn't set out to explore or explain the NHS in all its glory or faults. These are my memories and if you remember it differently, well, those would be your memories. Sharing my imperfect memories with you in this book was a promise I made myself quite early in my career, not because it's a good story but I hope it describes some of the situations I found myself in trying to earn a living to keep my family afloat.

In life, I got it wrong many times, misreading situations, saying the wrong thing and choosing the wrong option. I never got wrong who the good people were and I always cared for patients and my colleagues. It was hard not to feel saddened by some of the lives of the people I met.

I have witnessed and been included in some amazing conversations provoking thoughts on the NHS as an employer and care giver. It is an inclusive employer, with a fantastic workforce of every age group, I know of colleagues still working on the front line in their late 70s. The NHS has many highly trained and good-hearted staff, with so much to give to a system that often lets them down. When staff most need support, when they are at their most vulnerable, caring for their own family, the support just isn't there.

Society doesn't really value carers. I don't only mean those in hospitals, but those in nursing and care homes in community settings and those that care for an individual in their own home. Carers are often children and elderly saving the government millions. The financial and psychological consequences of caring for a loved one at home are huge. For me as a carer it was being forced into early retirement, six years before state pension age. You will read about one manager that wouldn't support me working two days a week when I needed to spend time with my sick husband. She wouldn't consider any reasonable adjustments to my full- time position. That isn't the NHS it is the work of a bad manager. The NHS gets slated because it employs managers with very little understanding of care and definitely no empathy.

I'm not alone two out of five carers struggle with working hours and financially. Carers can be emotionally shattered watching a loved one deteriorate day after day. Old routines and activities are gone, the chance to try new things diminish away daily. You become a planner, are there stairs, ramps, and good access to toilets, the list goes on. I wish for better support for some, good respite care for those that need it, and a proper benefit more like a wage for carers and that shouldn't stop after retirement, needing care doesn't stop when your carer retires.

The NHS employs a mixed bag of people, knowledgeable, proud, shy, a few with obsessive compulsive disorders, and some real bastards. I remember the absent-minded staff and those that were overly cautious. Some with learning difficulties and those in senior positions you just couldn't quite put your finger on, what was wrong with them.

Psychopath spectrum, not the killer sort but with impaired empathy and egotistical traits, that's what they were, many with egotistical traits.

A few managers worked with their teams and were present. I was prepared to follow many people because they created time for me, giving me access to training that helped my development.

Gossip, there was so much gossip. It was usually true. There are thousands of employees working in any hospital and within each of these is every kind of person you can meet in society. There were a few drug users I came in contact with; sometimes it would be the gossip you heard that would make you say "Oh that's why". The colleague arrested for stealing drugs, members of staff with alcohol issues and staff suspended for looking at porn and those who served a prison sentence. Numerous people put on gardening leave for inappropriate behaviour or some other reason that was slightly altered by the time it got to the shop floor, and yes most unfortunate information about staff got to the shop floor.

The thing is you don't remember the mundane the ordinary the everyday activities. You remember the unusual, the special, the sad, the illegal, and the doctor that got away with ...... yes, you should have been investigated and possibly prosecuted. Just the same as remembering all the good things you have done, it's very difficult, but you will easily recall the bad things you did or said. I am going to do my best to remember the ordinary and mundane sprinkled with a little of the unusual.

I can only portray my experience, sometimes seeing the bigger picture, always with an opinion and occasionally even a solution. I met many compassionate front-line teams guiding patients and families through stressful emotional times. I met managers good and bad, some that would recite Trust values like a prayer, others that didn't have a clue what the values were.

Even the language was different, if I attended meetings with a majority of Physicians, Surgeons and Nurses we would be talking about patients' their condition, medication, results, further treatment and family. When attending other meetings, you could play buzzword bingo, resilience, escalation, deep-dive, outside the box and gap analysis amongst other words were banded about, as if there was some deep meaning, or something really important was being discussed. Nothing complicated was really being said but it sounded good, you wouldn't hear the words patient, family, nurse or doctor.

I remember staff ringing in sick and witnessing them shopping in Manchester. The porter I met on the tram, who said "you haven't seen me" guilt. How would I have known he was skiving off. Staff sneaking out early, not an approved early finish.

There were always discussions at many levels

relating to getting it right, improving this, changing that. So much talk about the focus on the next new initiative, that had to be cascaded down to the wards, all in the name of efficiency, of course. Initiatives, repeated time and again, always familiar, "haven't we done that before" "no" this is called something else. Managers trying to reinforce their knowledgeability.

I remember conversations about moving patients at the wrong time and to the wrong place. Why did some managers consider their opinion more valuable than the clinicians? I don't know but they often did.

Why do we keep getting it wrong? I remember working on A&E with Junior doctors caring for medical patients, then we opened a medical assessment unit to beat the 4hour target set by the government, if the patient didn't arrive in A&E there was no target to meet. Diverting patient flow from one area because of demand doesn't decrease the patient numbers or change their needs for the service. You can move patients as many times as you like they will still require the same amount of care and resources. This move added another area, where the physicians would find their patients. Medical patients were placed on all wards within the large hospital, the physicians and their teams were regularly seen walking the corridors searching for them. What a time-consuming waste of energy, not just because of the minutes it took to walk between wards, the corridors were a meeting place and often conversations took place during the journey so the focus diminished. In the early days it was the same physicians seeing patients on the medical wards, in A&E and the medical assessment unit, plus the outlying patients on surgical and gynaecology wards on ICU and CCU.

My roles were varied starting as a nursing auxiliary/support worker on a gynaecology clinic and surgical wards. I then became a Medical Team Co-Ordinator (MTC) I loved this role, supporting Junior doctors on ward rounds. Managing and training the MTCs followed, by this stage I was immersing myself in as much education as I could. Attending college to learn how to teach and assess medical students, co-ordinators and nurses on venepuncture and cannulation, many more topics followed.

Through the hospital I achieved a diploma, Managing in Health and Social Care (MHSC). I joined Oldham Business School part of Huddersfield University and gained Masters level qualifications in Strategic Management and Leadership. Two Consultants financially supported my development with endowment educational funds, Dr Simon Hanley and Dr Martin Pattrick and I'm very grateful. Further education and training continued right through to my retirement; I was so lucky in this area.

I left my medical teams on the wards to manage a fantastic team who scheduled theatre lists in the Access Booking and Choice (ABC) department. I loved this group of staff, I couldn't do what they did, exceptionally fast computer skills, amazing underpinning knowledge of individual patients' requirements and theatre procedures. It took me a while to realise I didn't need to do, "the do", I just needed to manage the service, they were nice people to manage, very supportive of each other and of me. We were a multi-sited hospital and knew that the day would come when departments would merge. When this began my ABC team moved to Rochdale. I was missing the general hospital bustle and remember crying many times in that new department just wanting to leave, far too much politics and supervision for me. Julie Owen saved me.

I joined a Listening into Action (LiA) small team who were helping to bring about positive change for patients, staff and families. I remember the CEO met with us regularly to provide support and leadership, he seemed to be a real enthusiast for change. It was around this time I joined Mike's army with the Care Quality Commission (CQC) as a specialist advisor doing hospital inspections.

Our small LiA team were taken over by a Director of Quality Improvement, a lady with real underpinning knowledge of change models, which she shared with us eagerly. She was a real educator. The team grew to nine and we were just beginning to make inroads when there was another takeover and Salford management moved in.

My husband Vin has mega health issues which you will read about in this book. In 2017 I felt he was deteriorating and in August of that year my good friend Karen Feeley passed away very unexpectedly. Losing Karen affected me greatly, making me re-evaluate any time I was away from home. Then I heard my colleague Chris Pollard passed away too. A sad time for me.

The serious decision to reduce my hours to two days per week were being considered. I was mourning and worrying. At work we were dealing with a new manager with poor people skills and no compassion, you could see our team of nine becoming stressed and self-survival became important.

Through my thirty plus years I worked in clinics, on medical and surgical wards, in departments, within corporate and education & training.

I'm very grateful to the NHS and specifically to a handful who supported me. After putting together, a chronological order of roles, courses and qualifications, I realised every couple of years I achieved something. I gained new skills and qualification from basic care and information technology right up to Master's level. The training and support I received depended on my manager and a few colleagues who you will read about in these pages.

It all started in 1984 after the birth of my third child

and the death of my young father-in-law. My family moved to the same street as my husbands' mother in Salford. We jumped at an opportunity and bought a house. During this time, I fell ill and needed major surgery at Withington Hospital South of Manchester. After a twelve week stay, I was sent home to recover and began to think about work. My experience as a patient made me appreciate the care I received and I began to considered roles I could apply for within a hospital, rather than the secretarial roles I had been used to.

Working in the NHS wasn't even a flicker of a thought until that patient experience. I wanted a change and applied for two roles at a local hospital. Two part time jobs, one in the afternoon the other in the evening. I took both jobs.

VAGINA DAYS

Gynaecology Clinic –
Afternoon shift 12:30 to 4:30

I was allocated three cream checked dresses which fastened with poppers up the front, wear one, wash one, and dry the other. We all wore paper hats that folded into the standard nursing hat, held in place with hair grips. A few ward sisters wore cotton starched frilly hats and I remember one had cotton frilly cuffs to match.

The gynaecology clinic was held in an area shared by the maternity clinic based at the back of the hospital.

Every clinic had one consultant and junior supporting doctors usually a registrar or senior house officer. Every doctor was chaperoned by an auxiliary. Doctors were chaperoned for litigious reasons; hence my name being written in the patients notes.

There was one staff nurse, to be honest I wasn't sure what she did, she was a nice lady though. I remember a good WRVS in the waiting room for the patients. When called through to clinic patients were asked to pop a gown on, ready for their consultation. I worked with two consultants and one registrar each week.

One consultant played music during clinic, even asking what I was currently listen to. At the time Graceland's by Paul Simon was my preferred music of choice, the following week that was played in clinic. Thoughtful. There are other reasons why I liked this consultant; he kept me interested, involving me in conversations during his consultations, explaining symptoms and tests pointed to specific diagnosis.

We often had students join the clinic and prior to seeing patients' the consultant would discuss symptoms and test results encouraging students to come up with a diagnosis, occasionally he would ask me too. I became pretty accurate. I felt confident in his clinic. The medical students were often nervous of Consultants and I never understood why, mostly they were very nice.

At first, I was a little embarrassed seeing ladies in such an exposed position during their examination but that feeling dissipated within the first couple of clinics. While patients were being examined, one of my roles was to positioned the examination light for the best view of the vulva and vagina passing the consultant equipment like smear spatulas or silver nitrate sticks.

I always thought speculums would come in different sizes but if I remember correctly, there was one small speculum that was never used and the rest were all the same size.

When we were short staffed, I would work with two doctors running from room to room. One shift while working with a Consultant and a Registrar a patient was examined before I entered the room. I informed the Consultant not to document my name as being present, he must wait for me. I don't think he liked that, waiting for an auxiliary before he could continue, but he did.

Pelvic floor exercises were performed by me during every clinic mainly in response to witnessing patients suffering from urinary incontinence. During the examination the consultants would ask patients to bear down enabling them to look for descent of the vaginal wall or uterus. One consultant used a sims speculum (two blade sims, shaped rather like $\sum$ this) while patients were on their side it was the best for diagnosing a cystocele or rectocele and when the speculum was removed you could witness a uterine or vaginal prolapse. Asking the patient to cough was another tool the consultants used to diagnose incontinence, I witnessed urine form a rapid stream spurting with such force from the cough. You had to move quick.

Heavy periods were a very common presenting complaint and the patient would be asked a specific list of questions, e.g., how many sanitary products used in a day. Every complaint had a list of questions that would be asked. There was a lot of repetition in gynaecology I think the repetition was why I learned such a lot.

Patients requiring termination of pregnancy were seen on these clinics every week. Performing terminations is one of those truly horrible procedures the doctors do, and it must affect their mental health, yet you don't hear them talking about it. Ladies that presented for this procedure were not all treated equally. One doctor refused ladies for no other reason than they were the third lady they had seen that day requesting the procedure. These days were difficult for me, I really believe in fairness which you don't always witness. One shift I remember so well, we had a full clinic and three ladies presented for termination. The first procedure was agreed and a date set. The second lady in her twenties wore a suit and carried a briefcase, very work smart. She was in a stable long- term relationship and wanted a termination because it was the wrong time, both her and her partner worked. The termination was agreed and a date set. The third lady, around thirty with four children discussed not being in a stable relationship. A termination was not agreed. The patient left the examination room and I could hear her sobbing. I ran to the cubicles side of the clinic and sat with her for a while to calm her down. I gave her a number for a clinic in Manchester; she needed two doctors to agree a termination. I do hope that lady was OK.

When I returned to the clinic the consultant said "you think I made the wrong decision, don't you" I remember saying, "I don't judge either the patient or the consultant" that was definitely not my role.

There are a couple of very sad stories from this time, the young girl with learning difficulties who required a termination. I still remember my thoughts during that clinic, who got the girl pregnant? Were the police involved? Those questions were not asked in clinic.

One young girl came to clinic with internal testes she was born genetically male, but had the external appearance of female genitals. She didn't have a womb and would be unable to produce children but otherwise would be perfectly healthy and able to lead a normal life. I remember how sensitive and appropriate the Consultant was with these patients.

One patient arrived in clinic requesting sterilisation, she was young in her twenties and during her examination the consultant said "is there any possibility you could be pregnant", the patient said "no". To which the consultant talked about a cervix having a blue hue when pregnant. I didn't know if this was true or not, the consultant thought her cervix looked blue and asked me to confirm. I looked; I have no idea what I was looking at. The consultant then said, "I think you're pregnant". I want you to go home and make an appointment in one-months' time and if you still want sterilising, I will do a termination at the same time. The patient left the hospital, returning a month later, not pregnant, for sterilisation.

My thoughts were, the consultant was very clever in making the patient really think about sterilisation at such a young age. I still don't know if a cervix has a blue hue when a woman is pregnant.

When a patient presented with heavy periods, I would make comparisons with myself, for example, patients complained they were using four sanitary products a day, I would be thinking, is that all, I can use a packet a day. Other times patients presented with hirsutism, and one consultant regularly asked me to confirm that the patient had a normal amount of hair for a female. I have always been quite fair and I don't have a lot of hair, asking me was not a good comparison, as most ladies who presented with this were dark haired. I used my experience of ladies I had seen in clinic; none were too hairy. I feel sorry for the females of today they shave all their body hair, what on earth for.

One shift with a new female Registrar I prepared the room and called in the first patient. I prepared the equipment trolley while the doctor took the patients history and documented her presenting complaint. I helped the lady assume the position and returned to the trolley that was at the end of the examination bed. I opened the gloves and placed them and the speculum on the trolley. I held out the KY jelly to add a good squirt. The doctor didn't seem interested in the KY she decided to play with the speculum, this went on for a minute or so which is a long time when you're watching. There is a screw which opens the top and bottom part of the speculum and allows the user to view inside the vagina. The screw is turned once the speculum is inserted, that screw was twisted up and down, I don't know how many times. I thought all doctors working in a gynaecology clinic must be proficient using equipment, how wrong was I. The doctor turned to me and asked "can you do the examination of the patient".

I remember the look of horror on the patients' face, I made our excuses leaving the room, pulling the doctor behind me. I returned almost immediately and apologised to the patient. The doctor, sat on the corridor outside the consultation room learning how to use the equipment. I was ready for a huge complaint, but no, not that I was aware of. That patient also let that doctor examine her. Patients trusted doctors. God bless her.

The presenting complaints of most patients were common, abnormal bleeding, pain, discharge, incontinence, infertility and post pill problems. I remember the diagnosis of patients with cervical erosions, polyps, pelvic organ prolapse, endometriosis and fibroids. We saw cancer patients and the occasional lady who had a sexually transmitted disease (STD). I will never forget the look on the ladies faces when the penny dropped and they realised the STD was from their husband or partner.

Bastards.

During a patient's examination they would lie on a narrow bed with a pillow for their head and a short sheet to cover their dignity. A disposable pad was placed under their bottom. The consultant would stand at one side of the patient and I would stand on the other. Both the consultant and I would go to the busy end, when the examination and swabs or smears were required. Ladies don't like to be examined. Two examinations have never left my memory.

One lady grabbed my dress, which fastened with poppers up the front, pulling me towards her, as the dress popped open my breasts were fully exposed into the consultants' face. Neither of us expected this. Boobs visible to full extent, and mine aren't small. The consultant smiled and it was never mentioned again. I had a nice bra on, why do I think that makes it better.

The second examination etched in my memory happened when a lady grabbed my dress, knickers and pulled out my pubic hair. The tears rolled down my face, the consultant looked as shocked as me, that was never mentioned either.

We had a regular patient who arrived in handcuffs from prison. She was the first prisoner I met being treated at the hospital, there would be many more. I cannot remember her condition but I do remember her request, "rest", she always asked for a note excluding her from work, she always got one.

Other consultations include ladies with a missing tampon which created an offensive smell, ladies who suffered from a womb prolapse and had a plastic device called a ring pessary placed in the vagina to keep the womb in the correct position. Bloody awful, the things women have to put up with.

One clinic we saw a lady, post honeymoon with a small tear that wouldn't stop bleeding. Her husband attended the clinic with her. She was admitted for a procedure in theatre that afternoon. Her husband worked at the hospital and the consultant asked me to speak to the ward sister to ensure her details were kept private. I escorted the lady to the ward myself and only spoke to the ward sister. A few days later I was in the office of a male surgical ward where I worked after my shift on gynaecology. This is where I overheard staff talking about the honeymoon of a colleague, saying he had been so rough his wife needed stitches. I was absolutely furious and told the nurse they should be ashamed of themselves for spreading such vicious gossip.

This wasn't the only time I had to do this. One member of staff had a termination and that information was spread to those that would listen. Gossip can be very damaging.

I started to notice the number of patients per clinic

increasing and I was finishing later than contracted. It didn't matter how many patients were on a list but my finish time gave me a break before I started my shift on the male surgical ward. After a few months I made enquiries and discovered that the patients I had been seeing were private, everyone involved in their care except me were receiving payment. I stopped seeing private patients and staying late in clinic. I was later to discover this was common practice, private patients being seen in NHS hospitals using NHS resources like me for free.

At the end of the clinic the dirty jobs began, putting all speculums into a bucket, ready to be sent for cleaning, I bet they still do that, disgusting job. All swabs were sent to the laboratory including the Chlamydia swabs which were taken for research purposes. The swabs for this purpose were stored ready for use in the placenta freezer. One shift I noticed the freezer was unplugged, what a sight, no matter what I write it will not convey the sight of a huge freezer full of placentas, the colours red purple blue, big spongy, bloody, veiny and lumpy. I bet the contents of that freezer went into our makeup. Dread to think.

One of my saddest memories relates to a consultant I loved working with. He disappeared one day without a trace from the clinic. No explanation was given from management, gossip took over and there were many reasons banded about relating to his absence. I was told that he was frog marched out of the building because other consultants disagreed with his treatment plans. I have no idea if the gossip was correct or not. What ever happened, I don't know, he was a colleague we had a good working relationship we should have been trusted enough to give some sort of explanation, if only to prevent the gossip.

I seem to recall the oddest of things, the way someone spoke to me, sometimes I remember what they said but mostly it's the intonation and a feeling I remember. The most senior Consultant I suppose he would have been the clinical lead for the department or was it that I thought he was the lead, I never asked I assumed but I have poor memories of the way he spoke to me and my colleagues, dismissive and ungrateful not my sort of person. I gave him a few weeks and things didn't change so I had no respect for him, thankfully he wasn't one of the Consultant I chaperoned.

The nurses in the main hospital would occasionally say to me, "I know your face but cannot quite place it", let me reassure you we all look mostly the same. Seen one, seen them all. Not my favourite job the gynaecology clinic but it suited for the short time I was there.

LAUGHTER – GAS AND AIR

Surgical ward
Evening shifts 5pm to 9pm.

I began my evening shift on a male general surgical ward on the top floor of the hospital. From the first day and for the first month a ward sister short in stature took great pleasure upsetting one of the nurses. I met the nurse on the stairs as I began my shift. She didn't like the way the sister spoke to her. I would listen, try to calm her down, all the time thinking what I would do if the sister spoke to me like that. I didn't think I was suitable for this environment, coming from a secretarial background, I had no experience of bullying or any really bad attitudes from people in a work environment. I had been lucky. I would experience and hear of bullying during my career in the NHS.

Then I met a ward sister with curly red hair and a

huge personality Pauline Dorrington, I have no idea what happened to the nasty sister but I liked this red head. I met two nurses Geraldine (Ged) Mcloughlin and Debbie Drinkwater, I don't know if it was because I was new, or they really were the best nurses I ever worked with. They taught me the basics and I settled into my new role.

The basics in those days were to support staff nurses caring for patients, thinking back, it depended on the auxiliary, if you were capable, they would give you more things to do, and I loved that. There was no real training except for moving and handling which I received about three months into the role. I remember the Australian lift where you basically put the patient on your back. Lifting always affected your back, making that worse would-be nurses and doctors' that didn't put any effort into the lift. One two three and ... you were on your own. I didn't lift or move a patient with them again.

During my first week on a very busy shift, I was asked to observe a patient empty his colostomy bag. The patient, bless him, had emptied the bag once before but still needed moral support. Of course, "I would cheer him on". After a chat with the patient, I realised he wasn't very confident, but I was ready to give him as much encouragement as I could. He made ready the equipment and removed his shirt. I was a little shocked to say the least, why did the colostomy bag have to be see-through. The bag was attached to the patients' belly it was a roundish plastic bag with a straight section at the bottom. The bag was tied with a plastic clip; just like those you get from IKEA to seal packets of food. The patient began and as far as I was concerned, he was doing fine, I was doing my best poker face.

The first thing I remember was the smell, strong doesn't describe it, a toxic decaying pong filling the ward with a creeping acrid pungent haze. My next job was to give out the evening meals. Lovely. There I was expressionless watching a man squeeze poo out of a clear plastic bag. I won't say there was poo everywhere but it did get in places it shouldn't. He did a great job, and looked confident and pleased with himself, I felt I had done a good job too, I didn't react to the shock to my senses.

Over the years I realised that smells didn't bother me so much, sputum was going to be the thing for me. Later that evening I returned to the patient with the stoma, we chatted about my new job and his stoma, the first I had ever seen, we laughed as I thanked him for the experience. I believe stoma bags have improved and are designed to be more discrete so they are probably not see through any more. The nurse crying on the stairs stopped and I started settling into the first month of my new job.

My evening shifts began with a quick report on each patient followed by saying hello to everyone, it was a male surgical ward where I experienced good honest banter. Those men could have me in fits of laughter and I loved laughing.

One evening there was no one around to give me report so I went to say hello to everyone. There was activity behind the curtains of one patient, I heard "is that you"? I wasn't sure who "you" was, but said "it's Moira". There was no verbal response but a pillow flew over the curtain rail, landing on the floor. When I bent to pick it up, the curtains were flung open, and a clinical trolley covered in equipment was launched at me. The stainless-steel trolley had two shelves and four wheels. It took off, I don't know how she did it, but it flew, I caught it mid-flight. I stood there holding the trolley as two of the wheels fell to the floor. I couldn't put it down, I remember looking around the ward, it was quiet except for the weird noises coming from behind the curtain. I was staring at the clinical trolley covered in paraphernalia that I had no name for. I wondered if the, "is that you" statement meant I should have gone behind the curtains to help, but it was too late now.

A group of doctors came running on to the ward, all ignoring me with a trolley mid-air. I was surrounded by wheels and a pillow in the middle of the ward listening to the frantic happenings behind the curtain. The patients were doing their best to ignore the happenings, reading the paper sitting facing the opposite way on their beds. Then one kind gentleman put the wheels back on the trolley. I realised the patient behind the curtains had arrested, I asked patients if they wanted me to close their curtains for a while.

The activity and weird noises eventually ceased and everyone left except for one doctor, it was that doctor's responsibility to write in the patients notes. The patient hadn't pulled through. I didn't know the man who had died.

I was later asked to help a nurse prepare the patient for rose cottage (the morgue). I was happy to help but apprehensive at the same time. This would be my first experience of death but I didn't want to tell anyone, what – was I thinking; you have to get your experience from somewhere.

The nurse was amazing, so respectful and that stayed with me. I had to chat through the whole procedure because of my nerves, I chatted to the patient, I told him what we were doing and apologised for disturbing him. That chatting with the deceased never stopped it was my way to show respect and for coping. Are you wondering what we did, nothing much really? We removed all lines and covered the areas with gauze and tape. We washed the patient everywhere front first then back. Combed his hair and tried to put his teeth in with no success. We closed the one eye that remained open and wrote a buff-coloured label with his details on, which we attached to his toe with a small piece of string. We wrapped his body in a clean sheet and put another label upside

35

down on the sheet over his chest. We covered him with another sheet and rang for the porters to take him to Rose Cottage. When a patient is placed on a cadaver tray in the morgue, they go in feet first. If you pull the tray out the label on the chest is easier to read if placed upside down on the patient.

I was impressed with everyone that shift. As time went by, I realised that panicking (throwing pillows over curtain rails and launching clinical trolleys) and over dramatic people were not the best at portraying a good example of how to run an arrest. That I witnessed later with the doctor I called the conductor. He was a registrar when I was working with the medical teams, he led many arrests at the hospital. The conductor would stand at the end of the patient's bed and give instructions to everyone in attendance, they were the best run arrests I ever witnessed, clear instructions spoken and repeated back, if you were not doing something you shouldn't be there, people left, it was calm, organised, giving the patient the best chance of survival. Well, done to you, all I can remember, you were blond, not as tall as me and a union representative for the doctors and I loved watching you work.

The weeks and months passed by and I loved my new role. Nothing was too much trouble. I was good at this job; you see when you become a carer it changes you; I cannot say how or why but it does. Maybe being a carer heightens your empathic natural passion for helping people. I was enjoying caring for patients and liked the people I worked with. The memories of a few patients stayed with me and for many different reasons.

A consultant told a patient he had an ulcer but I heard a different diagnosis in report. As time went by, I forgot to ask why the consultant did this, was he saving the man from the news he had cancer, surely not, he wouldn't have been that arrogant to prevent the man from setting his life and death in order, was it that he thought the man couldn't understand or want the information. The patient should have been allowed to make his own choices about his last months. Still don't know why the consultant made those decisions but I wasn't present in the conversations the consultant had with the patient so maybe he didn't want to know and I was being hard on the consultant.

Mr. N D you were very sick not expected to survive and loved a bath. I gave you a bath every shift I could. I didn't need help you were lighter than my children. At first you struggled with your diagnosis and kept asking me when you were going to get better. I had no answer for you, but we would chat about the day and things you had experienced, you would listen to me chatting about my young family. I can still see you to this day. I wasn't there when you passed away and I remember being sad but knew that was something I would have to get used to.

37

We are all going to die and we don't know where or when, there is no place on earth where death cannot find us. We can ignore death while we live or we can confront the prospect of our own death. However, we cannot overcome it. All we can hope for is that our death is in a place of our choosing with people we love and that love us. In a hospital it's never quiet, it's very public often dramatic, the nurses do their absolute utmost to make it as comfortable and stress free as possible. Many people want to die alone and wait for their relatives to leave the room for a coffee, then they slip away. Families watch and this can be very traumatic for them. People die at any time of the day or night in side rooms and on the main ward, the family often look at the nurses to do something but there is nothing to do and that is difficult to see.

I considered it an absolute honour to sit with and care for the dying, I would sit and wonder about their lives, who they loved and who loved them. I do not remember one not even one patient that I thought was wealthy. Was it the catchment area for the hospital, I don't know but being rich to me wasn't about money or things you have its about relationships and family supporting and caring for each other. That is probably why I never noticed any wealthy people I just don't consider wealth in the same way. That is my wish for everyone, I always hoped the person I was sitting with had a wonderful family of friends who loved them and would miss them.

That first winter I remember wanting to shout "where's the soap" the day I fed a foul-mouthed patient. He was neglected and thoroughly miserable, he didn't want to eat or in fact have anyone near him. He was quite young and very vocal. It took such a long time to feed him often visitors would arrive on the ward, (no open visiting in those days) I wasn't giving up, I was told to feed him and I did. He called me every abusive word you can think of at the top of his voice, "you bitch, you fxxxx cxxx", I'm not a prude but from a generation that finds really bad language offensive, I mean, if you can think of anything worse, he shouted it. One of the nurses shut the curtains on a particularly bad day, as if that made a difference, what the visitors thought I can only imagine, and if their imaginations are as bad as mine, there would be terrible scenarios being played out in the visitor's minds deciding what I was doing to him. This went on for a while and eventually he began to feed himself. I'm not sure what was wrong with him surgically, but he left that ward a healthier weight and my ears did recover eventually from the onslaught of bad language. This was my first experience of bad behaviour in a hospital, I didn't know that there would be many more to come.

One patient being treated for a bed sore arrived at the ward on an unusual bed, it was shaped like a boat and filled with what I imagine to be moving sand under a blue cover. The bed was electric and when caring for him it was turned off making the sand solid. There was a platform on either side of the bed for us to stand on while treating him. This was the first and worst pressure sore I ever witnessed. The wound on his bottom and lower back covered a large area it was deeper than a clenched fist. The dressing was poured into the wound and it set like a sponge. The patient never complained, even when he was manoeuvred into the most degrading of positions to pour in the dressing. I wondered how this could happen, neglect.

My confidence grew, I was enjoying my busy job, there was little or no time to sit around. The ward was busy and during visiting hour I would sit with a patient that didn't have a visitor just to listen to their amazing stories.

Nine months in now and Christmas arrived with decorations and a large tree at the end of the ward. One of the Junior doctors was playing Father Christmas on the day and all patients had a gift wrapped ready for them, the usual was talc or toiletries. I remember diaries being bought one year, how inappropriate for very sick patients.

Staff brought in food, there was always a buffet on the go. I remember a nice atmosphere, as many patients that could go home went home, leaving us with around twelve patients. During the Christmas period hospitals always attempted to slim down not only staff but patient numbers too.

There would be the bare minimum of doctors and nurses to deal with the really sick that couldn't go home and the elderly that had been dumped with a vague complaint allowing family members to spend a few days with no caring responsibilities.

Sherry for the patients' wine for the staff (a very small glass). We moved the beds and the TV to the middle of the ward. On the lead up to the big day staff were going for a drink in the evening, this wasn't a regular occurrence, like you see on the TV programme Casualty. I was working with the sister on the late shift, night staff arrived early so we could join the others. Our patients, in particular one chap had been with us for such a long time, sister thought he would benefit from a break away from the ward; he jumped at the opportunity and enjoyed his beer that evening. We had to sneak him back in through A&E as all the other doors were locked at night. He loved it, Cheers. I liked that sister even more for that act.

One evening shift around Christmas I was putting dirty laundry for collection onto the corridor when I noticed a female trying to drag a male along the floor. There was only one door after the ward and that was the doctor's mess. I shouted "what are you doing", a young distraught face looked up at me. My god, what a shock they were doctors, I never really thought about doctors and their social lives. There was a Christmas party in the mess and what a mess the floor littered with food, paper cups and bottles.

41

The furniture was strewn with what looked like teenagers. I closed the door behind me after helping to put the junior doctor on one of the sofas. Little did I know I would witness plenty of drunken doctors in the future but not within the hospital building. That was probably one of the last parties that took place with alcohol in that doctors' mess. They knew how to party.

There was a nice atmosphere on the ward, everyone did their best to make Christmas enjoyable for the patients. When the tree was looking bare, we knew it was time to take the decorations down. On the late shift there were three of us, the ward was at full capacity with over twenty patients. I cannot remember why the nurse was off the ward when the sister asked me to help her get rid of the tree. I thought it would be collected from the main corridor but she was concerned the pines would be all over the ward, which wasn't hygienic for a surgical ward. We opened the fire exit door onto a metal walkway which took you to the next block. Metal open corridors from block to block. They were generally used for patients who sunbathed in the summer and for emergency use in case of fire. Patients often had a tan if they were with us over the summer. We dragged the tree to the walkway, I thought we were leaving it there. No that would be a problem if there was a fire.

Up the tree went and over the top of the hand rail landing with a thud two storeys below. We could have killed someone. I didn't look down before we pushed the tree over, I assumed the sister did. We stared over the rail to the broken tree below when there was another thud. The fire door shut, now that shouldn't have been a problem, but we couldn't get back in. The door jammed, it seemed frozen. The ward now had zero staff. We waved and shouted at people we could see, mainly patients, I'm sure one patient waved back at us. Eventually we were heard and the door was opened. What a relief, I was just glad we hadn't killed anyone. I think the ward bought an artificial tree the following year.

One of my roles was to help patients returning from theatre, popping them back into bed, popping on their pyjamas. Most patients just went back to sleep for a couple of hours. Nurses used the word POP to describe many activities, pop to X-Ray, pop on the chair, pop to theatre, patients and staff popped everywhere.

Having the giggles one evening, quite common for me in the early days, I helped a patient post theatre. I hadn't met him prior to surgery and his procedure was lengthy, he was quite groggy on his return to the ward. A couple of days later, the patient was sat up looking much better when I heard him say "you're the lady that tucked me in after theatre, I remember your laugh." That taught me a lesson; never assume anything when you think a patient is not aware.

I must have been a happy person in those days because I remember a lot of laughter, maybe I became too serious as the years went by, I don't know.

I was asked to shave a male patient from nipple to pubic region. OK, off I went with a razor, shaving foam and a small aluminium bowl for water. My goodness he had more hair on his chest than I had on my head. He was going to theatre and needed to be ready in minutes. I was very gentle and he giggled every time the razor touched him. There was hair everywhere. The porters arrived and Ged (favourite nurse) came in and looked at the mess. She didn't say a word; she disappeared coming back with talc and three razors. She sprinkled him with talc and after a few quick no messing strokes she had finished. The patient and I just smiled at each other. God bless Ged my no messing fantastic nurse.

Helping an elderly frail patient take a bath one shift turned into the biggest clean up ever. A colleague helped to transfer the patient from wheelchair to bath hoist (a toilet seat on wheels), then she left me to it. I turned the handle raising the patient high enough that his legs wouldn't catch on the side of the bath. Before I could wheel the hoist over the bath, he asked for the toilet. I began to lower the hoist, he began to open his bowels, diarrhoea.

He was half over the bath with his other half over the floor, it was everywhere including me. On the window ledge lay a stack of cardboard bedpans and I grabbed them but couldn't separate them, I just pushed the pile under his bottom to catch the poo that didn't stop. I managed to pull the emergency cord and summon help. The nurse, looked as shocked as me as she entered the bathroom. Together we put pan after pan under his bottom. He was embarrassed and began to cry, I felt like crying too.

We put him at ease, we could deal with this. I had to empty the bath clean the room and wipe him down before I could even think of lowering the hoist. While I cleaned, he was wrapped in a blanket still sat on the hoist, finally he was clean enough to lower into a large bubble bath. I have never seen that much poo; he filled three bed pans to the top I thought he might go into shock. I later found out he'd been given picolax (a laxative). That was another pair of shoes ruined. I went home in those hospital plastic flat slipper things and borrowed theatre scrubs.

Most patients recover from their surgery and are discharged home and I found that a really positive experience, witnessing a person in pain, suffering, then recuperate and leave the ward with a big smile. This didn't happen for one patient; he was in hospital for about a week before his surgery from which he was recovering.

We made a good connection, he joked and I laughed through many a shift, then one day he had a stroke, which affected his movement and speech. At first when we were caring for him, he looked confused and depressed.

One evening with Chris another of the nursing auxiliaries, we were laughing as we entered his curtained bay. He did his utmost to communicate pointing and grunting, he made us understand, "are you laughing at me". I was mortified that he thought, we would do that. I suppose my expression was a shock to him too. That patient then gave me a one-sided smile and put his thumb up, he was joking and trying to tell me he missed our banter, I missed it too. He worked hard every day to regain movement and speech, at first it was staggered and spluttery but there, if you gave him enough time you could decipher short sentence. The jokes soon came and we were back to laughing and joking with each other. Nice man.

At meal times a large trolley would arrive at the entrance to the ward. The trolley contained trays with plated food. Not all wards were the same, some wards received their patients' meals in a smaller heated trolley and the ward staff would plate the food. If you worked at the hospital, you were not allowed to eat patients' food. All nursing staff did, either in the office or in the shared kitchen.

When patients had finished eating, their trays were collected and placed back on the trolley. Patients occasionally removed their teeth or glasses and put them on the food trays. Why, I have no idea. To be honest I never checked the contents of the trays unless I was documenting how much the patient had eaten. There must be a black hole of teeth and glasses, rather like socks from washing machines, as patients often didn't get them back.

One lovely Jewish man told me amazing stories, like most people I loved to listen to life stories and this patient had many to tell, he was a magician and took great pleasure telling me where he had performed and his favourite tricks. I told him my young son loved magic. I don't know how he found my address, but one day there was a knock at my door, and there he stood with a magic set for my son and a work cardigan for me. What a lovely gesture.

One evening I was asked to collect medication from a psychiatric ward. I remember writing the name of the medication on my hand, I knew I would forget what to ask for and I had no idea where the psychiatric wards were so decided to follow the signs but couldn't find any. There were no signs for the psychiatric wards in the main hospital, I had to resort to asking. Eventually I found the ward and pressed the buzzer to enter. It was difficult to distinguish between patients and staff; everyone was smoking and there wasn't a uniform in sight.

A lady smiled at me, I moved towards her and requested the drug written on my hand. She was lovely, very chatty and took me to another woman, the nurse, who gave me the drugs. Patients and staff were sitting together smoking and drinking tea it was more like a social club than a hospital ward, so different from the clinical areas I was working.

Smoking in hospitals was very common in the early days. Both patients and staff smoked in toilets, in the canteen and outside in the grounds. I remember a patient setting their locker on fire during a time when smoking was banned from the toilets. Patients couldn't always get to the smoking area, they lit up in bed and as nurses passed, they put the lit cigarette in the locker. Eventually one caught fire. If you banned smoking in the early days the smokers just moved to another area. I remember catching a patient smoking in one of the linen rooms. Staff often used the sluice, large windows and plenty of cleaning products to disguise the smell.

As time went by my nursing role began to expand and I was asked to perform more and more qualified nursing tasks. Neuro observations was one of these responsibilities, it was performed on patients and involved different tests including pupillary reaction. I was asked to perform these on one of our patients. With pen torch in hand off I went and completed the task.

Everything was normal except one of the patients' eyes was glass. When finished I went back to the nurse and didn't comment until she asked "was there any improvement". I said, "all observations were normal and one of his eyes was glass". I thought I was wrong; she took me back to the patient, to look at the chart. Two previous recordings found two normal eyes. That was the first time I realised there was an issue with the way one of the student nurses documented, basically she copied the error of the previous nurse. The patient did have a glass eye. The nurse talked the student through correct documentation and recognition of glass eyes. I thought it was obvious. I bet you are shocked that an auxiliary was asked to do neuro observations, I was surprised at first, then it became normal practice.

Auxiliaries performed most of the direct care that involves patient contact, we took care of all aspects of daily personal hygiene, performed observations and prepared equipment for example we set up the clinical trolleys for procedures. We took down dressings and removed cannulas, ordered stock and checked the oxygen and suction. We prepared those that passed away and hugged their families. Most people have no concept of the role of the lowest paid person looking after their family member, until they are admitted to hospital.

One evening shift I was asked to go and help at another hospital; they were short staffed. It was a small local elderly hospital, a short drive away. This wasn't unusual in those days, hospitals in the locality helped each other in desperate times. Sister said a taxi would take me and bring me back. My evening shift started at 5pm and after our discussion and waiting for the taxi I arrived at the small hospital at around 6pm, I would spend three hours there. It was meal time and most patients needed to be fed, I was asked to take over from a male nurse feeding a patient. I was shocked at the speed patients were having food spooned into their mouths. A few patients were quite flat in bed and I worried they might choke. It reminded me of a mother bird feeding her young. The food was all pureed, no chewing just swallowing and then the mouth opened again and another spoon full was put in, all too quick for me. I watched as the staff went from patient to patient. I chatted to my lady and waited in between each mouthful. I was told to hurry up. I had no intention of rushing a patient and continued at a slower rate.

The next shocker for me came when all the dinner plates had been removed, the staff went from patient to patient getting them ready for sleep. The lights were turned down, the ward became quiet, it was seven o'clock. I asked what they did next; we have a break then answer any calls, basically sitting around for two hours.

I felt uncomfortable putting patients to bed so early. Were they really poorly, no they were just old. If staff had taken their time to feed the patients while chatting, those two hours would have had a really nice effect on the residence of that ward. I didn't see any senior staff during this shift and made my complaints to the red-haired sister who said it would be dealt with. Who knows if it was or wasn't? I wasn't asked to go to that hospital again.

One male patient I remember had to use gas and air while having his dressings changed. I couldn't imagine having to use that as a painkiller for a dressing until I saw his wound. I was dirty nursing during his procedure, he had undergone a vasectomy that had become infected leaving two pockets in his testicles. He had been to theatre to debride the sloughy necrotic tissue. Every couple of days he had his testicles packed with ribbon gauze soaked in iodine to encourage healing and reduce the risk of bacterial infection. You should have seen the amount of gauze used to pack his testicles.

Barbaric jobs like packing wounds, nurses do every day and is crucial for tissue growth at the wounds base to prevent premature closure of the wound and the formation of abscesses. Awful procedure for the patient, however nurses seem to relish picky poky prodding activities, like picking spots.

There were some awful operations performed on patients on this ward, I remember one patient that had an oesophagostomy (an artificial opening into the oesophagus) for cancer. There were discussions where the nurses said big people take longer to die and he did, bless him. I have no idea if that statement is true or not. One patient had a drainage bag attached to his neck so food he chewed would go straight into the drainage bag. Awful.

Emptying drains and catheters was one of the activities I did most evenings. Once emptied I documented findings on the charts at the end of the patients' bed, the volume and colour of fluid, plus results of dip sticked urine. Every drink and bag of intravenous fluid was documented on these charts. The ward had good charts, most if not all staff were conscientious about completing them. I later learned other wards were not as thorough and some nurses couldn't add a column of small numbers.

Most days we managed to get a break away from the ward and spent twenty minutes in the staff canteen. The best part of any break was the chat and getting to know other people you worked with. We had both female and male nurses and I learned quite a bit actually. It was OK to be different not all females wanted children or to be married or to be promoted, ward management wasn't for them.

One nurse wanted to work in IT and after a couple of years he left nursing and eventually became head of that department. We discussed our homes and aspirations. Occasionally I bump into nurses from this time and we reminisce as they were good times.

There were a few awful operations I don't have a name for but remember the consequences and suffering of the patients. My overall memory good caring people looking after fantastic patients. They taught me how to care, setting a good standard for me to follow. Most of all I remember the patients', and laughter. Every nurse on that ward was excellent and very professional. I would be happy for any of them to look after me or my family and that stands today more than thirty years later.

In 1988/89 the Whitley Council introduced a new grading system for nursing staff with grades between A and I. A and B were for unqualified nurses and health care assistants and grade I was for nursing officers and matrons.

That was a very stressful time, listening to staff almost fighting for the senior roles, even the auxiliaries. I do this and you don't, was the main mantra. I left both the gynaecology clinic and the surgical ward at the same time to work full time on a female vascular ward, I didn't look back.

THEATRE DAYS AND TEETH

Vascular / General Surgical Ward – Full-time

The female vascular nightingale ward had twenty-two beds and was based on the ground floor of the hospital. It didn't take long to realise the ladies would be harder physical work than the male ward. I swear the ladies left their bags at the door with expectations that would not match the service we could provide, "can you plump my pillow, pass the water" – when they could reach it themselves. It took me a while to adjust to the routine and characters I met on this ward. This was a full-time role in one area so I began to work the full shift pattern.

The rotas were produced a few weeks in advance using a request book where staff document their preferred days off and late shifts. The occasional rota created a debate about who works with who and conflict about days off. This ward is where I experienced routine, theatre days and ward rounds.

Nothing appeared to be too much trouble for the nursing staff and I quickly settled as the standard of care was good. The operations and conditions treated included amputations, ulcers, all vascular and general surgery.

The patients that stayed the longest were amputees and we really got to know them and their families.

The ward was run by two sisters very different in character and the way they treated staff. The senior sister (the ward manager) was relaxed, in fact almost horizontal, she liked office work and spent a lot of her shift there. Although she may have been absent from the ward work for most of her shift, she always handed out the patients' meals especially on a late shift which saved me a job. I would watch as the food trolley entered the ward, it took about one minute before she was up and handing out the meals, probably to ensure she received the meal she wanted. She was a very supportive manager to anyone with personal problems and at one point or another we all had those moments in our lives.

On more than one occasion a nurse from another ward would pop onto the ward to do a haircut for this sister, not on a patient, but on her in the office. The nurse would arrive with equipment from her old hairdressing career, it didn't matter what was going on outside the office. She was having a trim and that was that. Doctors and nurses were in and out of the office during these appointments, I was surprised she got away with this, hair clippings get everywhere including wounds and this was a surgical ward. Wow, the things I remember, she never stopped snacking and cutting her cuticles with a stitch cutter. I did like her; I remember asking if she needed turning one shift as she hadn't moved out of her chair.

The junior sister was a different kettle of fish and my memories of her are marred by unfairness to untrained nurses. Auxiliaries were known as untrained nurses, and a few trained nurses loved this; it would be their mantra to affirm seniority. The junior sister insisted in giving trained nurses extra perks, an extra day off with pay, of course. Auxiliaries would not get that opportunity.

One Christmas after working the major days without complaint, she authorised an extra day's annual leave for all nurses for working hard over the holiday period, I said "that's really nice" her response was "it's for trained only". I lost all faith in her as a leader and don't remember one decent conversation with her after that comment, she was elitist. Hey ho it takes all kinds of people. She was popular with some nurses, maybe it was my expectations, I believe in fairness.

There was a matron at this time over multiple wards

who supported the sisters in times of management difficulty. I remember her telling me that she used to ring a bell from the office to call nurses, my thoughts were, you better learn my name as I won't be responding to a bell. Cheeky cow.

Matron was called to sort out rota problems one shift as all auxiliaries requested the same weekend off. My request was for a family wedding and to be honest I had worked quite a few weekends compared to the others, at that point in time. I remember matron in the office with the junior sister. What are they up to! (Any time the office door was closed everyone thought decisions were being made about them, when usually it was someone having a quiet moment alone or a chat with a friend.) After a while the auxiliaries were called. Matron informed the group none could have the weekend off. I informed the matron I would still be attending a family wedding and if the previous rotas had been checked she would know that I hadn't had a weekend off in months. Compare it with the others. I left the office. I was not afraid of challenging management.

Later the matron said all auxiliaries will be working that weekend except Moira as she hasn't had a weekend off in a while. Nice one Matron for listening. Junior sister you should have looked at the old rotas in the first place.

Theatre days were so busy and we regularly missed our breaks due to the activity on the ward, it also depended on who was in charge. One particularly busy theatre day a patient had passed away; another had returned from intensive care and others were returning and going to theatre.

The ward manager asked if I would do her a favour and sort out the patient that had died. I went behind the curtain to collect a bowl from the locker when I noticed the patient had a central line, catheter and drips still attached. The central line is sewn into the skin, the catheter is held in place by inflating a balloon within the bladder and the patient had a saline drip attached to her arm. I returned to the office to report my findings; the sister passed me a stitch cutter from her draw and said "use a syringe to deflate the balloon in the catheter". She was confident in my ability to perform this task and I was confident to do it.

I collected gauze, tape and a syringe from the clinical room and went back to the patient. Notice where that stitch cutter came from, sisters draw in the office, she kept a box there for her cuticles. I filled a bowl with warm water to wash the patient and went behind the curtain. I removed the cannula first covering the site with a small piece of gauze and tape. I then began to remove the dressing from the central line when a doctor came behind the curtains and asked what I was doing,

"What do you think"

as I held up the stitch cutter. He said "I haven't certified her dead yet; we have been too busy in theatre for me to pop down to the ward." I replaced the dressing and left the doctor with the patient. I cannot tell you how agitated I was, I know the patient was dead but you still feel it's wrong. I was furious at the sister; she was really quite calm; I wanted to throttle her for being irresponsible putting a new member of staff in that position. The doctor came into the office and told me I could continue. Now it sounds terrible but from the patients' perspective she had passed away and was left comfortably in bed for well over an hour. Her lines and catheter were removed; she was carefully bathed and wrapped with dignity and the greatest of respect by me.

One particularly awful winter when personal problems were discussed at most breaks, husband dying, mother dying, two husbands leaving wives; one nurse molested in her own home, brother dying, miscarrying first baby. Concentrating on anything was difficult.

I remember sitting by a patient getting emotional with tears running down my face. I was concerned for my own problems. Further down the ward another nurse sat by a patient visibly upset, I noticed the response from the patient with whom she sat, care, comfort and a cuddle.

Shanti the senior sister asking both of us if we needed to go home. No, we needed to stay and learn to cope, and we did. Long-term patients knew us, we were like a second family.

One of the reasons I loved that ward we were such an amazing team, very supportive of each other. Well, done Shanti for supporting your staff through such terrible times. We had some shockers, that year girls didn't we. We asked the Rabi to come and bless the ward at Jewish New Year, we needed any help we could get and our Jewish friends came and blessed the ward when they could.

Once a week I would play hairdresser taking ladies to the bathroom and giving their hair a good wash and do my best to set it in rollers. Once dry and with a little backcombing, they were done and I was ready for my next client. Two things I remember about this, the patients chatted to me as they would a hairdresser, we talked about holidays, would they suit a fringe or shorter hair. I'm sure the patients found this therapeutic.

One particular day I noticed a patient had head lice but I had been washing her hair for weeks, with no lice. I came to the conclusion we had given her nits. I remember checking the hair of staff and patients that shift. The nurse spreading nits was very grateful for the free nit service that afternoon.

We must have been one of the smelliest wards in the hospital as some patients had gangrene, foul brownish pus, rancid rotting heavy smell you never get used to, anaerobic bacteria along with necrotic tissue. We plugged a machine in near patients with stinking wounds, the patients weren't aware the machine was for their wound smell, it did take the edge off though.

Necrotic tissue had to be debrided, one practice I found difficult to watch, such a picky prodding activity picky, picky, picky. To this day it gives me the shivers just thinking about the task, I avoided dirty nursing for most debriding procedures. Nurses on vascular wards deal with this every day, there was a lot of this on that ward. I remember nurses correctly identifying bacteria in wounds with a sniff, they would say "that's staphylococcus it's a bit cheesy and they were right.

Each week there would be a dressing check by the consultant and his team. Prior to the team's arrival the nursing staff would remove all dressings and cover the wounds with a sterile paper towel.

One particularly warm summer, Angela Phillips one of the nurses was removing the dressings from patients on one side of the ward and I was doing the same on the other side. Angie started shouting for help. Usually, it would be a stubborn dressing stuck to the wound of a patient, we would pour saline over the dressing to loosen it without causing damage to the healing skin. I went behind the curtain to join Angie with a handful of saline sachets to see her struggling with wriggling maggots that had escaped a dressing. Now these weren't disinfected maggots that had been put there to clean out necrotic tissue, these soft bodied legless larvae, of a fly had been laid when the wound wasn't covered. They did the trick though; the wound was really clean but Angie didn't want to upset the patient by letting her see them. How awful, but to be honest that patients wound was the best it had been. The consultant was very pleased and I remember him saying if only we could prescribe maggots. Apparently, they can now.

Very occasionally a patients' toe would fall out of the dressing when it was removed. I witnessed this once and remember looking horrified as the toe was wrapped up with all the rubbish from the dressing and put into the bin. What did I think would happen to the toe, I don't know? Vascular nursing is such a traumatic job, diabetic patients losing their limbs, ulcers that never heal, pain with the limb and post amputation still pain. You need excellent nurses on a vascular ward and B1 had them. Doctors and nurse have to be strong to withstand the shocking things they witness. To remain caring and humane you must not allow the daily suffering to drag you down into apathy or depression.

One of our regular young female patients suffered with severe leg pain was eventually listed for amputation. She must have had terrible pain to want this, her leg looked normal. I will never forget her time in the hospital. She was brave even starting the amputation group with Amanda one of the nurses. I hope the group exists today.

One of my favourite responses to an operation happened when a young woman was admitted for breast augmentation, her breast shrivelled post pregnancy. On her return from theatre, I watched as she looked down her gown, I witnessed the beaming smile grow on her face. That was one of the nice operations you could see how it healed and lifted her spirits.

One late shift I noticed an unconscious diabetic patient sat upright in bed, thankfully the pillows were supporting her enough, stopping her falling to the floor. She was clammy with a white/grey pallor. I pressed the emergency bell and the ward sister came running from the office. I tried to rouse the patient enough to get her to sip a drink with glucose in. The on-call doctor assessed the patient and gave her a bolus injection, plus a drip which continually monitored her condition. That was the first time but not the last time I would witness a patient experience a severe hypoglycaemic episode, and it was quite frightening, I thought she was going to arrest.

Things went wrong as they do everywhere humans have an input; a needle was left in one patient's leg. One lady went to theatre with abdominal pain and returned with a tube up her bottom, she had wind. I remember laparoscopic cholecystectomies were offered to patients instead of open cholecystectomy, we worried about the patients that had the laparoscopic procedure as the surgeons were learning and the procedure took much more time than the open operations.

My memory of one surgeon in particular sticks in my mind; he would enter the office before his ward round and expect the nurses to bleep his junior team. We all did this; he never bleeped his own team or in fact have much of a conversation with any staff on the ward. I thought he was quite rude. One day I was in the office alone doing filing and the surgeon arrived on the ward. I must have been in a bad mood because I decided, if he wants me to call his team, he will have to ask. He stood there while I carried on. Neither of us spoke. Eventually he left the office. I bet he didn't know his teams bleep numbers or how to dial into the system. I still don't know why he didn't ask though. One of the theatre nurses was having an affair with this consultant. Gossip, everyone knew, I'm saying everyone knew because they always did. I know of affairs that have continued through two marriages and are still going on today they think nobody is aware when in fact most people were.

I remember husbands and lovers visiting patients at different times, I thought what complicated lives people lead.

The day room on the ward was a hub of activity in the early days, patients watched TV, ate meals, played games, we even called bingo there. The room was full of large chairs, foot stools with the odd drip stand in the corner. One afternoon there was a commotion in the room, I arrived at the door to witness two elderly women fighting. Yes fighting. One woman with dark hair in a bee hive style rolling round the floor with another patient. I cannot remember the other patient but can recall watching the bee hive disintegrate as the hair clips fell out. What a sight. I shouted in just the same way I would shout at my children, if they were being naughty. I had to help them up off the floor. What a sight. Such bad behaviour, I have no idea what set them off.

Theatre day arrived and our routine was getting patients ready in order of the theatre list, clean patients, shaved if required, no nail varnish, paper knickers, pop a gown on, take your teeth out. What was it, in those days everyone had false teeth? We worked down the list, we didn't get the patient ready too early. Everything was timed including the tablet to relax the patient prior to them leaving the ward.

Two ladies that day were in beds next to each other. The porter arrived putting the trolley next to the patient. We pumped the bed up to the correct height for the porters' trolley and pulled the curtains round. The patients would pop on the trolley, we would cover them to preserve their dignity and keep them warm while travelling down the hospital corridors.

The ladies were in theatre and I prepared for there

return by folding the covers to one side of the bed. Each patient had a bed side cupboard and a table on wheels. On each table would be water, a plastic beaker and personal belongings, like their teeth in a denture pot. Of the two ladies, one was about seventy but looked much younger and had expensive looking false teeth. The other lady in her forties looked much older with teeth full of debris. Oh god I remember this well, I still heave. The first lady back from theatre was the youngest, I helped her back into her nightdress and pulled the closest table to her bed. I opened the pot of teeth and she popped them in her mouth. She mumbled the words "these aren't mine". She had a beautiful set of pearly whites in her mouth. I knew what I had done, the patient removed the teeth and popped them into the pot, I gave her the other denture pot and she popped the teeth straight into her mouth. I heaved, I wanted to clean them, she was adamant they were fine. I gave the good teeth a clean ready for the correct patient. Imagine if I had put the revolting teeth into the mouth of the older patient, I dread to think. Gives me the shivers. We all make mistakes. The patient trying the wrong teeth didn't complain she didn't seem concerned.

I experienced more cardiac arrests on this ward than my previous ward. That was nothing to do with care but the condition of the patients. Staff dealing with cardiac arrests were all very different, either absolutely fantastic or rather panicky, human nature. We supported each other at these times. I cannot remember in the early days' resuscitation being discussed with either the patient or their family but then I wasn't privy to those sorts of discussions. If a patient was not for resus, it would be documented in their medical notes. This occasionally got missed during report. Three arrests stand out to me.

A patient at the far end of the ward arrested. At the office I called for the crash team when a senior nurse ran past me and off the ward. The nurse behind the curtain was doing compressions on the patients' chest. I pulled the bed away from the wall and removed the head board while the nurse continued. Everyone responded in the usual way except for the senior nurse that ran off the ward. She was going for the crash trolley when porters normally collected it. She forgot to unplug the machine, she ran towards the door pulling the electric socket and cables from the plastic casing along the wall. She was ripping the cables out as she ran. The crash team and porter arrived before the crash trolley. She was panicking and always did in times where she felt stressed.

A state enrolled nurse (SEN) was covering staff absence one shift, she normally worked on the high care unit and was very experienced but in theory the most junior nurse at that time. During the morning a patient arrested, the call went out for the crash team, followed by screams for help from a very senior team member wanting the SEN to take control. Not a good example to set.

On returning from break one shift, I found a patients' husband crying on the stairs. "What's happened", he told me his wife had died and they were resuscitating her and she will die again. She was not for resuscitation and very sick, a senior nurse called the crash team. She did pull through the arrest and died later that day. I realised these memories were created by the same team member. It has to be down to training surely as this was a senior member of the team.

One of my best memories of that ward was working in pairs making every activity enjoyable, we chatted making beds, washing patients, doing dressing and while dirty nursing. Chris was my favourite for working in pairs, she was so funny and made me laugh usually at her family antics.

When making beds a platform of metal bars would be pulled out from the end of the bed. The platform held the bedding while the plastic covered mattress was washed. One shift I fell over the bars but held my weight swaying on the metal structure. My legs were bruised and I was in pain for months, even today my skin feels different over that area. Chris was laughing, until she saw the state of my legs. Incident forms were not promoted in those days, I don't remember anything ever being filled in.

Sundays was cleaning day for vases and equipment in the sluice and bathroom.

Suction and oxygen tubing were checked. We used lots of sterilising tablets, we couldn't use bleach. The cleaning was done where the smokers congregated for a sneaky cigarette. Lots of nurses and doctors smoked in those days, I still remember the ICU consultant who seemed to have a cigarette in his hand or hanging out of his mouth at every opportunity.

Toast, there was always toast hot and cold in piles on every ward for all the patients and staff. One of the auxiliaries each morning would make piles of the stuff, cheap bread and even cheaper butter.

Occasionally auxiliaries had more experience than qualified nurses, an example of this happened when I was the dirty nurse, assisting a trained member of the team catheterise a lady. I often thought I was there more for morale support for the nurse rather than any other reason. She was obviously having great difficulty, when I looked, she was trying to catheterise the patient's clitoris. I pointed this out and later told her to get a mirror and have a good look at herself.

One afternoon a young woman waiting for surgery was quite aggressive and I recognised her anger related to pain, I too had experienced uncontrollable back pain and remember ringing A&E shouting at some poor nurse "what else can I take" as I had swallowed more than the recommended amount of pain killers. The patient was begging the nurse for pain relief but the nurse said she couldn't have anything else for another two hours. I remember asking could she have another kind of painkiller.

In the early day's auxiliaries did the drug rounds with nurses, gaining experience that could be passed on to junior staff. She locked the drug trolley and went to ask the doctor. Thankfully the patient was prescribed another type of painkiller and she went to theatre that evening.

On the 1st April 1990 there was a Majax (major accident/incident) announcement over the Tannoy informing staff to consult the major incident folder on their wards. "Do not ring switch, follow the instructions in your Majax folder". "Where's the folder", the hunt began. "Moira see what's going on".

The first person I noticed was male wearing brown overalls, with a truncheon hanging from his belt. The truncheon was longer than the ones the police used. He stood on the main corridor, leaning against the wall. Empty trolleys lined the wall on one side of the corridor, we were expecting lots of patients. Our ward was close to A&E and it was the first time I had seen so many trolleys waiting for patients. The corridor was quiet, I made my way back to the ward, the folder had been found.

Eventually, we were told of a riot happening at a local prison, it was the Strangeways riot. Prisoners had taken control of the chapel and the riot spread throughout the building. Suspected sex offenders had been beaten and were arriving at the hospital. I would say at that point anything else I heard was unconfirmed gossip but the terrible things I heard ranged from mutilation of private parts to throwing prisoners off balcony's was very distressing. Being on the female ward saved me from the trauma of that event.

During afternoon report nurses were asked to volunteer to show a patient how to use a urethral dilator (Urethral dilation stretches the sides of the urethra, the tube that carries urine from your bladder. Sometimes scar tissue from surgery narrows this.) The patient needed to use dilators post sex change surgery. There wasn't one volunteer. I have no idea why nurses saw this task as more difficult than the picky proddy activity they did every day with wounds. Judith eventually volunteered, she was the most senior staff nurse in the office that shift, so I suppose she didn't have a choice. She asked if I would accompany her, we went to see the patient. I pulled the curtains round the bed and turned to witness the patient, lay, legs akimbo saying "looks good doesn't it". I was shocked to see a woman very happy to expose her private parts. I found her question difficult to answer, neither of us responded. My thoughts were very different from the patients, I was used to the gynaecology clinic and ladies opened legs but not to an extent they were exposing their innards. I thought the results of her surgery were different from vulvas I had seen. I don't know if that was because the surgery was incomplete and she needed further operations. I didn't ask I felt it was too private a question. When I got to know her better, I thought she had mental health problems. She had strange behaviour and would say very odd things. Over the years I met other patients either waiting for or having a sex change. One young man waiting for surgery, had a lovely soft face and a real problem with alcohol and drugs. He was often seen begging for cigarettes in the staff canteen or sleeping in a chair with a bottle of methadone next to him. I always wondered what happened to him.

Certain patients stick in your mind for many different reasons, mostly as I said before it was because they or their situation were unusual. One morning I couldn't rouse a young woman from sleep she wouldn't open her eyes or communicate. She stayed in bed all morning not moving, eyes closed, observations absolutely fine. I remember the psychiatric team visiting the ward to do a consultation, followed by her transfer that afternoon to their ward. She came back to us as bright as a button. I believe they gave her Electroconvulsive therapy ECT in which a small electric current is passed through the brain. Apparently, it causes changes in brain chemistry that can reverse symptoms of certain conditions. Sounds awful but it worked for her.

The old ladies often had names for their private parts many used the term tuppence, cookie, flue, fancy bits, and velvet. Others used male names like Arthur, why didn't they just use vagina or vulva.

I saw awful tattoos in private places, arrows pointing to vulvas, mild and bitter on breasts weird shaped animals all looking worse for age and gravity. While patients were being examined, our heads would turn to the side as we tried to work out what the tattoos began life as. We never commented and occasionally acknowledge with a nod, that we had identified the image.

The side room was often used by dying patients as the main wards were always so noisy and very public. My recollection of the people in that side room isn't the patients it's their families and the occasional staff member post-surgery. Comforting patients' partners and listening to them talk about them and their life together. I remember one couple they didn't have children and I drank tea with her husband most days, I took care of his meals as he stayed with his wife for her final days. One afternoon a nurse reported smelling smoke and on investigation I found the patient in the side room had passed away and her husband was having a cigarette. We turned the oxygen off and opened the window. I sat with him until other members of their family arrived. He just held my hand and I sat there.

Every day auxiliaries can be found sitting with dying patients, holding the hand of a family member or a patient while they passed away. Auxiliaries provided a lot of comfort to patients and families. Sitting in close contact during someone's final moment is a humbling experience and a reminder of what we all have to come. I have many memories of families and how they coped in the first moments of pain of loss that overwhelming feeling after losing their loved ones to death. On my emotional days I would find it difficult not to sob with the family other times I was able to distance myself a little. You just never knew what would upset you and everyday was like that.

Answering a phone on a ward was always an issue and we all had a responsibility to respond to the calls. Every day around ten in the morning we received a call from the patients' kitchen, this call was always a waste of time. How many meals? any special meals? Every day that call came and every day we received a menu for each patient to make choices for the next day. We never had empty beds so on the whole we needed twenty plus meals. The supervisor of the kitchen insisted he spoke to the ward sister and she would insist he spoke to one of the nurses. I refused to get the ward sister and informed the kitchen of anything different but it was rare that there was a change, we always had meals over patients didn't want to eat or couldn't because they were too unwell, it didn't matter that supervisor was adamant he wanted to speak to the sister and she would confirm no change.

Most calls came from family members checking on the condition of their loved ones, these were easy to respond to as all staff received a good report before each shift. When I answered one call, I didn't have a clue how to respond. The caller wanted the amputated leg of a patient that had been on the ward and had now passed away. To this day I cannot remember who I called to deal with this request but apparently, it's a thing that can happen for members of the Jewish faith.

There was one thing we practiced on B1, that I didn't see on other wards, wash bowls being offered to patients before a meal or after using a commode.

Most mornings I would see a lady carrying an old-fashioned handbag going to see her husband, we chatted about the weather and nothing. These meetings went on for months, I never questioned or asked how her husband was, because she hadn't told me why she was visiting the hospital, I had assumed.

Then one day I met her on the neurosurgical ward where I was covering a gap in the rota which was quite common, nurses from one area being moved to another area because of staff shortages. I never really minded moving; it was a good way to see how others worked. I arrived during report and slipped in the back of the room. Rita one of the sisters acknowledged me with a nod and I listened to the sad reasons' patients were there. Just as I was about to leave the office, I noticed the old lady with the handbag, she was talking to the doctors and moving towards the office, she stood next to me and smiled, I said "hi, what are you doing here" I'm the neuro surgeon that works on this ward" I was speechless, what an unassuming lady and I later learned a genius.

Although I never witnessed it, I believe she was the consultant that took her sheep to work in her land rover and put them through the CT scanner. Occasionally you would see sheep in the car park.

Neurosurgical wards were not for the faint hearted it was hard physical work as well as emotional. The patients needed regular turns and you needed to rely on your colleagues to work with you. Starting at one end of the ward, when the turns were completed, it was time to start again, like painting a huge bridge by the time you get to the end you have to start again. I remember spending so much time feeding patients through nasogastric tubes, food and medicine syringed down the tube into the stomach. They are the only tasks I did on that ward, turning and feeding patients.

I don't remember much banter, breaks or cups of tea on Neuro the work was stressful and hard. The staff were nice, it wasn't a good place to work, well not for my back or my wellbeing.

One young man admitted after a motorbike accident was ventilated and his wife and new baby were at his side. I was asked to feed their baby while the family were taken to discuss the young man's prognosis and possible organ donation.

He was brain dead. I don't know what was said or if the family agreed. I had lots of questions that shift and I don't think they were all answered. How do you approach the topic? How are the organs removed? Are you really sure he's dead? That was my last shift on neuro.

While covering on another female surgical ward the sister asked me to help her with a patient who was very drowsy, post theatre. I noticed something wrong with the manner of this sister who stood opposite me on the other side of the patients' bed. Respect, she didn't have any for the woman that lay there sleeping. She pointed out with disgust the patients' large belly mouthing "Oh my God look at the size of that". That was the first time I really saw a nurse be so disrespectful to a patient, I was shocked to hear such words from a person that I had witnessed as a good nurse.

Typing this has reminded me of a surgeon that called a male patient fat. He was a young body builder, just muscle and I remember a male nurse telling the consultant "I will let him know when he wakes up". The consultant wasn't impressed. I didn't meet many staff with such awful attitudes to patients and I bet they wouldn't recognise themselves as being rude.

Urology wards seemed to suffer most from staff shortages and I regularly found myself working there especially on theatre day. The patients often returned from theatre with a huge bag of fluid washing out their bladders. Clots would form in the tube and it would get blocked. Our job was to fold and twist the tube squeezing it to dislodge the clot. We called it milking; I thought it was a terrible description and it hurt your hands.

I remember being stunned the first time I was shown how to put a macradon on a male patient, this is probably a trade name. A macradon was a condom with a tube at the end. You attached a urine drainage bag to the tube, this helped patients with incontinence. The nurse told me some patients were quite old and finding their penis may be difficult. She was right many of us struggled.

Some men have a shortened or retracted penis common in the elderly or those who have had treatment for Prostate cancer. When the penis retracts into the scrotum it can be difficult for the nurse to apply the sheath. Some nurses were better than others at this job, putting pressure on the pubis helped the penis protrude and if you were quick the sheath could be applied and a tape added to prevent it slipping off. I remember thinking you're kidding you want me to press there and grab his penis. "Yep", and as calm as you like she put the sheath on the man no messing. I couldn't believe I would be expected to do this and to be honest if I saw a retracted penis, I would hope the nurse that taught me was on shift so I could ask her to do it. It isn't like putting a condom on an erect penis, I can assure you.

A cardiorespiratory technician regularly visited the male ward to do ECGs, she wore a white dress which everyone knew was see through, an underskirt was required. She wore a dark thong no underskirt. The male patients named her the thong thing and took great pleasure watching her walk and bend down. No comment.

Over the years staff went on strike a few times for different reasons. The decision to strike in an understaffed hospital was never easy. Surgeons wheeled their own patients to theatre, very few staff left their department or ward to strike, those on the picket line were on their day off or annual leave.

Three strikes come to mind, but there was possibly more that I don't remember. In 1988 thirty-eight-night nurses went on strike about unsocial hours. In 2014 staff from eleven unions did a four-hour stoppage due to pay. In 2016 doctors went on strike over a controversial proposal to bring in seven day working contracts. During a strike, reporters would be found at the entrance of the hospital trying to get stories, they managed to get into the building on a couple of occasions and staff were told to refer them to the communications department at the Trust.

While working one shift I met Myra a lady working on the bank, she had a good reputation. One of the sisters on a medical ward had offered her a full-time position. She was pleased as punch and jumped at the opportunity. However, she had a problem with writing and the sister discovered this and decided she didn't want her working on her ward. I remember the sister as being tall, stern looking and very starched. I later discovered she told Myra "To return to bank work" no reason was given. That auxiliary lost her pension, I hope the sister didn't realise the consequences of her request.

In the early years I wore a cream checked dress and staff nurses a pale blue checked dress. When the uniforms changed to white dresses or trousers suits with coloured epaulettes, it didn't take long before you could see who washed their whites with the colours, the white dresses stood out amongst the odd grey ones. The uniforms came unhemmed and the sewing room would hem your trousers, jackets and dresses. Unfortunately, the unhemmed uniforms were not quite long enough for me. I wore my dresses unhemmed and the fabric was overlocked to prevent fraying. My trousers and jacket had to be specially ordered for a longer length they weren't the best fit or the most comfortable or practical, I preferred the cream dress.

Students often came to wards for work experience, to be honest you were lucky if you could identify who was a junior doctor, a medical student or a school pupil on work experience, there was no difference they all wore white coats. Two girls were to join me for the week, two medical students. It was a busy surgical ward with an annex and they were to help me in the annexes part of the ward. They washed and dressed patients, emptied colostomy and catheter bags. I taught them how to do observations, they did them and I checked for accuracy.

They were very good and a week later we received great feedback and I discovered they were on work experience from school not medical school. I bet they are working in the NHS now. Things changed as time went by and work experience students were monitored thoroughly and their activities planned. Yes, auxiliaries did observations along with many other qualified nursing activities.

Rumours were rife relating to haunted wards, most nurses knew another nurse who had experienced something or other. Areas of the hospital did have an uncomfortable feeling about them, I put it down to the dark where you always see shadows, the chill at night and the tiredness of staff. I have been more spooked out in other situations than I have at any time in the wards at the hospital. My last job I sat at a desk in a very old building of the original hospital and I was often the first one to arrive. Now that office had a presence it didn't bother me and I never really mentioned it, there was occasionally a very strong feeling a person was in very close proximity behind my chair. Curiosity got the better of me, I put a mirror on my desk facing the area behind my chair hoping to get a glimpse of whatever made me feel uncomfortable. It will still be there and it's still an office, I wonder if they notice. I never saw anything.

Matron shouted me from down the corridor one afternoon, I thought what now, when she reached me, she asked "what has happened to your leg". "Nothing" I replied. Have a look its black. I looked down and a varicose vein had burst. She took me into her office and put a compression stocking on my leg, I went back to work. It has never burst since but aches occasionally.

It might surprise you to learn that when you became an auxiliary there was no formal training. You were interviewed and if successful given a start date. At interview I was told I would be trained but the first training I really received other than fire and moving and handling was years later.

The basic training was passed on by nurses rather like the doctors see one do one teach one. A nurse would show you how to do something and with no underpinning knowledge you performed the task. Mandatory training eventually began to cover other subjects in a little more depth.

The yearly fire lectures were awful, we had the same fire officer and the same talk year on year. The first time I attending one of his sessions I recall him saying, "If you don't pass the quiz at the end of the session you won't get a kiss". Horrified at the thought I shuddered; the kiss was a sweet. God, that went on for so many years.

Moving and handling in the early days wasn't the best training, no wonder nurse got bad backs. Nowadays they use hoists, I believe the NHS could have done much better looking after its staff. Funding and training have always been an issue for nurses. How can nurses leave the ward for training if its understaffed, which it was most of the time. Moving and handling should be done with the team you work. Team training and teamwork is very important for all staff on every ward.

From day one auxiliaries were thrown onto the ward and you just hoped for the best. Things changed with the National Vocational Qualifications (NVQs). The senior sister on B1 encouraged and supported me to take part in a pilot training auxiliary nurses to become health care assistants/support workers. The ward was piloting the course and paperwork. A new way to train staff, cheap labour really. I achieved my NVQ 1 & 2 very quickly with the help of Pat one of the staff nurses. To achieve my goals, I was allocated the first three patients on the left- hand side of the ward to look after. Other than giving medication, I provided all care. The nursing staff and sister had excellent supportive skills and I was very grateful to them.

Just after New Year, all staff completing their NVQs went to Booth Hall Children's Hospital for training. A male nurse providing one of the sessions asked how we had enjoyed our New Year celebrations. He had drunk way too much on New Year's Eve to be working an early shift in A&E and he had very little sleep. He recounted a young man running into the department shouting for assistance. The team ran outside and witnessed the young man's father had arrested in the car. The team worked on his father and were just about to give up when one of the doctors noticed he had made a little effort and began resuscitating him again. The nurse mentioned he felt sick doing the compression on the patients' chest. The patient survived and was later transferred to ICU.

Alarm bells were ringing, I said

"Was his name Aubrey", and the nurse went bright red. Aubrey is an uncommon name and my husband's uncle was Aubrey. I visited him in intensive care and didn't think he would pull through.

I turned to the nurse

"You were working under the influence of alcohol and had very little sleep when you treated my uncle".

I was so angry; I cannot remember what he said. My relative survived a very different person to the one that went into hospital, but he did enjoy a few more years with his family. This was not the only family member being cared for where I was present during a conversation that distressed me more than a little.

At the end of an early shift, I walked home. After a late shift my husband would pick me up. He would stand at the top of the ward and wait for me. The ward would be quiet, getting ready for the night, around eight forty-five. I loved this time where the ladies were settling for the evening. The atmosphere changed completely at this time of day, calm gentle and quiet, everyone spoke in a hushed manner, the main lights were reduced and a stillness would fill the air. The nurses would be giving handover to the night staff while the auxiliaries looked after the patients on the ward. Definitely my favourite time.

I had been working at the hospital for eight years and worked with some amazing people on surgical wards. I came across bullies and staff that looked down on auxiliaries, it was time to move on. I was successfully interviewed for an auditing role out of the NHS.

That same week I received a letter from the Trust asking if I was interested in joining a pilot working with Junior doctors. I had to complete an application form with an accompanying letter on how I kept up to date in the NHS. The application had to be in the following day. The criteria for the position were a minimum of four years' experience as a nursing auxiliary, two years on an acute ward and NVQ qualifications at level two. Those criteria reduced the number of staff able to apply and I assumed that all staff in the hospital with an NVQ 2 were sent that letter.

That evening, I completed by hand my application and typed a piece on how I kept up to date in the NHS. I had no other information on the role, there wasn't a job description, but what I heard sounded good and it was a higher grade a Band 3.

I discussed with as many people as possible what the job description would look like. There were many conflicting ideas being voiced, but the only true information from the discussions were of a supporting role to help Junior doctors. It was a government initiative to reduce Junior doctors' hours because they worked eighty-three hours a week, no wonder they were struggling.

I received a letter to attend an interview and remember arriving early, I'm always early. Sat there was an auxiliary from one of the medical wards, a shy quiet lady with visible nerves. The door opened and a candidate came out of the room. The nervous lady was called in, twenty minutes later, she left.

The interview room was cluttered, quite distracting really. Dr M Pattrick a consultant physician, the resuscitation trainer for the Trust Maureen Ryan, head of training and development (forgot his name) and a Mrs. Lyle Director for surgery at the Trust sat there waiting to interrogate me. My first thought was WOW so many senior people to interview auxiliaries. I remember everyone asked a question and I confidently answered them. Mrs. Lyle from the surgical area asked the toughest question.

I wittered on until I thought she thought it was answered. I left the interview after almost an hour receiving a message later that week, I had the job. I was happy and utterly terrified as I still didn't have a job description or a real picture of what the role would be. I declined the auditing position and confirmed I would be taking the position of Medical Team Co-Ordinator (MTC).

The surgical wards taught me how to work in a caring environment, how to communicate in stressful situations, care with compassion and on the side of hope. Respect and encouragement, generosity and concern, all aspect of my auxiliary and support worker role.

Many elderly and sick people find themselves in a position where they have very little contact with others. Someone to chat too, to hold their hand or put an arm around is very important. I remember when my mum was in a nursing home curled up, deaf and blind with arthritic pain on every movement. All she wanted was an occasional hug, it wasn't difficult to wriggle my arm between the bed and her back and snuggle into her neck. I missed a hug too and watching her smile was such a pleasure, auxiliaries do this every day. Providing that human contact is such a privilege and so comforting to a patient during a difficult time in their lives.

Thanks to all auxiliaries/support workers for the laughter, and sharing the load.

I had learnt and now fully recognised that a hospital is a teaching establishment, learning to be a surgeon, medic or nurse is an apprenticeship. Even after you qualify you join a lifelong learning school, a hospital. Doctors and nurses learn from each other aspects of care within their field. I witnessed seniors who led by example, shared information and knowledge to arrive at diagnosis and treatment plans. I worked with wonderfully skilled staff during my time on the surgical wards.

Working my notice flew by, I left to begin my new role as a medical team co-ordinator. I didn't look back.

I didn't drive in the early days and remember constant cloud cover and rain when walking to work, forty-five minutes of walking then seven and half hours of work, plus my house and children to organise. I don't remember much time being left over. We lived in a terraced house two working adults with three children, low pay, no benefits and very few luxuries. However, the days of not being able to afford bus fare for two adults had gone, my husband Vin used to cycle behind the bus, he helped me on and off the bus with the children, he always arrived at our destination before the bus. Vin eventually started to work at weekends to bring in extra cash and that money was used for little luxuries like the occasional nights out and we bought our first car and had our first holiday.

Our first holiday

Me and my buddy Chris

The vascular nursing team from B1
Tracy, Heather, Chris, Me and
Judith, Claudia, Jean, Josey and
Sheila

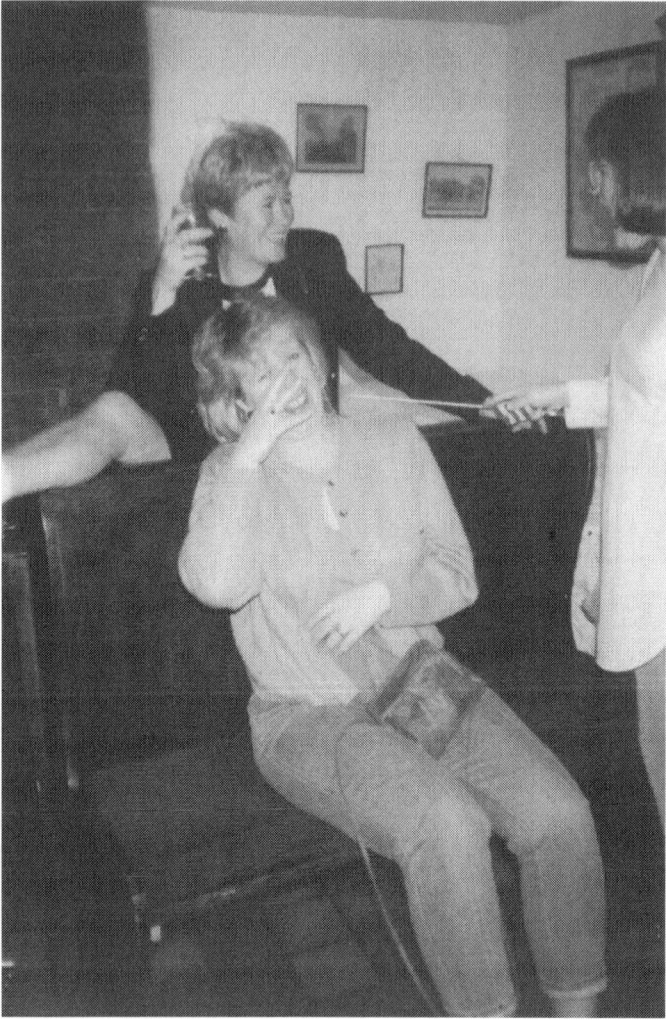

Chris, me and Amanda

Chris, Judith and Jean
Angie my sauna friend me and Amanda
I miss those sauna days Angie

THE DIAGNOSIS

It was around 1993 when my husband Vin an engineer started to feel clammy and said he had a bubbling sensation in his chest. His first recollection of this feeling happened while fitting security cameras at a shop in St Annes Square in Manchester. A chest X-Ray revealed widespread fibrosis and a referral was sent to the Infectious diseases department at the mother ship.

However, before we received an appointment a nurse called at the house to inform Vin he had TB. The department of health had been notified as the condition is a reportable one. We were really shocked to receive a diagnosis this way.

Vin could spend time in bed at this point he was so unwell and occasionally the GP would visit him at home. One particularly bad day I had to call the out of hours GP, I remember opening the door to a beautifully dressed doctor wearing a ball gown which wasn't zipped up, leaving her back exposed. I recall almost pushing her upstairs, she was so unsteady on her feet, but our stairs were steep so I'm going with that excuse. On another occasion a locum GP called one morning, he went into the lounge where my husband was sat and rather than say hello and chat about his symptoms he said "do you have Aids you know HIV" that locum left our house faster than his legs could carry him, not because he asked questions but his general attitude and lack of bed side manner was very poor.

Vin was diagnosed with sarcoidosis not HIV or TB and was referred to Dr Hanley a Respiratory Consultant. I wonder if his TB status stayed on the Department of Health data base.

This for me was the beginning of my worry years where hope seemed to fade as the months and years passed. The hospital consultants that saw Vin were fantastic but none of them gave me the hope I was desperately seeking. That reassurance we all want to keep us strong and fighting when loved ones are ill.

MEDICAL TEAMS

On my first day as a MTC (medical team co-ordinator) I reported to Maureen Ryan a woman with dark unruly hair and a wonderful Scottish accent, she always wore black, flowing skirts and tops. I arrived clutching my letter of appointment. Maureen was calm, knowledgeable and very supportive. That calm exterior was something I aspired to, but never achieved.

Maureen's office was small, off the main thoroughfare of A&E, we compacted like sardines into that space, anxiety levels high, virtually palpable. It didn't take long before Maureen calmed us all down. I'm saying all, but it may have just been me that was anxious.

I had no idea how many MTC had been appointed, firstly, there was Pat Phillips a tall grey-haired confident woman who liked to speak her mind. She was possibly the most vocal in the early days. I put Pat first because she appeared to be the natural leader of the group, she was the most outspoken. She'd been working nights and was a union representative which suited her very strong personality. Her knowledge extended to knowing exactly the details of this new role and where she would be working. I wasn't going to mess with her. I loved Pats knowledge of the hospital and I later learned she had a very big heart and would give you the sugar out of her tea, if she thought you needed it.

Jackie Eaton had been working nights on neurosurgery. She had grey spiky hair, the trendy one of our group. Over the years I realised Jackie like me needed to be kept busy and had a problem if time wasn't filled with work of value. Pat, Jackie and me spent many a Friday evening in the Same Yet pub in Prestwich drinking our way through bottles of wine laughing and reminiscing about these days, we still do. Pat and Jackie turned out to be lifelong friends providing me with great support and words of wisdom. Pat and I had many disagreements which were a good development opportunity for me, she was an avid reader and often read reports I wrote to check my grammar. Jackie turned out to be the workaholic of the group and a person I admired for having that calm exterior.

Sue had dark-hair, a similar age to me, with a very unique walk, rather like a speed walker, slow motion you know that hip movement, holding in a poo. She had been working in rehab. She knew how to keep under the radar, often having a sneaky fag.

Finally, there was Ann who worked on the Infectious Diseases (ID) department, she was another woman not afraid of speaking her mind. My thoughts were Pat and Ann would be hard to get to know they were outspoken and confrontational. I hated confrontation. As time went by my active avoidance of conflict melted away, I realised a certain level was inevitable.

Think before you speak, was the hardest for me. I never quite got the hang of that. Wearing my heart on my sleeve and offering my views early, still gets in trouble today. Some conflicts I witnessed were because people weren't listening and the focus was on personality rather than fact or event.

Maureen was trying to revive the knowledge we had, increase our confidence and with hope and training she assured us, we would be successful. A job description didn't exist, we discussed the roles and how we would fit into the consultant teams.

We talked about a training program which was written on the back of a fag packet. We had a convenient name for the role but weren't sure that was correct. We kept hearing complaints, the title of co- coordinators belonged to nurses. The name was changed a few times and for the purposes of this book I will use one of them doctors' associates (DAs).

On reflection the programme was done on the hoof, success come from our strong personalities, work ethic and determination to succeed, nobody else made this role successful, but the group.

Maureen told us we were to change the culture in the hospital. "You have to be strong; you will meet many that will feel challenged and threatened by your role" She was right so many were threatened by the role and that highlighted to us how insecure some very senior members of staff were.

Not knowing what culture changes really meant was difficult, especially as I couldn't recognise the situation being described to me. I had worked with nurses and doctors for years and on no occasion had I felt something was wrong with the culture. Management always quoted a bad culture being the overall problem.

Maureen was saying the bad culture related to blame and secrecy. The mantra that senior clinicians knew best and their knowledge was power seemed true in the early days. There were many unwritten rules within each team, specialty and department, lots of unspoken values. When I finished work years later my last role was in quality improvement and everyone was still talking about a toxic culture and still getting it wrong.

The teams and specialty cultures exist. The specialties Surgeons, Medics, nurses and Midwives share a common goal, they are supported and encouraged by likeminded colleagues. Expecting band three DAs to achieve a culture change within each team, specialty and ward was setting us up to fail.

We didn't fail, we became valuable members of medical and nursing teams joining multiple cultures over two very different hospitals. You can be part of more than one group, team, department and hospital as loyalty of one culture doesn't mean dislike of another.

Maureen said we frightened her a little. The group were strong women, yes, we were quite opinionated, some showing their colours earlier than others. Prior to our appointments, consultants were asked about the role and how supportive they would be to it. Of the consultants showing the most interest, five were chosen. We were asked if we had a preference.

Pat and Ann knew exactly who they wanted to work with. I didn't have a clue about the consultants, I hadn't heard of any of them. Which I thought was good, because I hadn't heard any gossip.

Pat wanted to work with Dr Pattrick the physician who interviewed us, he specialised in Rheumatology and was leading on this new way of working. Ann was adamant that Dr Dumbar an ID consultant was her choice. I cannot remember if Jackie had a preference. Sue wanted to work with the surgical teams. I wanted a change from surgery and was allocated to Dr Hanleys team in respiratory medicine. Jackie was allocated with another ID consultant and Sue to one of the surgeons. I can still remember the faces of the women when Maureen informed me, I was working with Dr Hanley, their faces displayed relief that it wasn't them. I never really worry about personality if that was what they were referencing in their facial expressions, I always make my own mind up.

In the first few weeks we shadowed our new teams. Not to do anything but to watch what they did. God, there was so much walking and I mean miles a day on top of my normal walk to work, with a pedometer I was walking about ten miles a day. Our patients were spread throughout the hospital on all wards. This was where I noticed the difference between the surgical and medical wards. Medical wards had older patients much heavier work for the nurses, it didn't take long for me to realise that these wards would not be anything like where I had been working. I very rarely heard laughter it was all quite sad. I felt sorry for the nurses on medical wards they didn't seem to have the same relationships and giggles with the patients that I had with the patients on surgery.

Sue didn't like surgery and swapped to medicine to work with Dr Klass and his team in gastroenterology.

There was one place for a further DA and Amelia joined the group. After her initial training nurse management for surgery stuck their noses in and took over her training and operational management, there must have been a problem and the role in surgery fizzled out. Just as Maureen had suspected.

We were back to five. Lots of training days with Maureen, a wonderful teacher who filled everyone with confidence. We covered resuscitation, heart, lung and ECGs all her specialty. At first, I didn't find the subjects easy, I didn't understand the theory enough to give me confidence, was I beyond learning. A Junior doctor qualified in dentistry and training to be a Max Fax surgeon spent days with us teaching resuscitation and intubation. Although we knew we weren't going to intubate, the exercise was to build our confidence.

As the days passed and the repetition of subject matter continued it became a key learning aid for me, repetition was working, putting knowledge to perform skills into my subconscious, practiced and rehearsed the information became easier. It took me a while to realise, I wouldn't be left behind, because I assure you if I hadn't been up to scratch, I would have been asked to return to my previous position.

Going out onto the wards wasn't going to be easy, some staff felt threatened and were having discussions about our group. The gossip was rife, we were taking over aspects of nurses, doctors and clerks' roles, all untrue but the pack mentality took hold and the gossip began to gain traction on the grapevine. Occasionally we would all be sat together laughing at the comments and gossip we heard. Maureen decided "get them out of uniform and document that they cannot be managed by the nursing team or they will be absorbed into another nursing type role" how astute was she.

The consultants agreed we were to be line managed by Maureen, accountability for our work sat with the Consultants and indemnity was provided by the Trust.

We wore white coats with yellow epaulette and I remember loving the pockets. I think we all did and when our uniforms changed, we seemed to ask for big pockets. Stupid, I know but pockets were important to us for some reason. The nurses complained about the colour of our epaulettes they were changed to a light green. They complained about the coat and the fact we were issued with stethoscopes and ophthalmoscopes. We were even stopped on corridors asking about the contents of our pockets; I remember replying condoms to one query.

There were complaints we cannulated feet, when in

fact the cannulas were for tests within the X-ray department, as though we were inserting them for the fun of it. Not only did we have to break down barriers, we had to put up with unconfident staff asking inappropriate questions. I believe the complaints came from one or two quite senior members of staff who took great pleasure trying to shut the role down.

Maureen knew exactly what she was doing putting us right in the centre of everything. We were to base ourselves in the doctors' mess, "they have to get used to seeing you as part of their team," she would say. As our lockers were moved onto the corridor within the mess other issues were raised, doctors pay mess fees and after discussion with the mess president we were given the OK and our fees were wavered.

The mess had two large lounges and one poorly stocked kitchen. There was a handful of bedrooms for the on-call doctors with one shower and one toilet for all Junior doctors. Ridiculous.

One lounge had a TV and large sofas. The second lounge, the smokers' room had a pool table. We ate our lunch in the smokers' lounge, the friendlier of the two rooms and to be honest most juniors met there.

The DAs had quite a reaction from the first group of doctors, "what are you doing in our mess" "who said you could eat your lunch in here". We always had an answer, we had learned to use the names of the consultants we worked with, a sort of shield. Name dropping became common practice, it implied the consultant was always right and the juniors wouldn't challenge the consultants, and we knew that.

If we had name dropped Maureen it wouldn't have worked, she wasn't a higher authority in their view. I became really good at name dropping in the first few months, always referring queries to Dr Hanley, in fact I told him if I became ill, I would insist on seeing my brother and I would name drop him there too.

Interest in the role was growing and other trusts were keen to meet us and discuss the groups progress. We visited a hospital in Sheffield doing a similar kind of role but not based with the medics they were ward based.

I was photographed for a piece advertising the role in the Manchester Evening news. The article read:

"TIRED JUNIOR DOCTORS WIN CUT IN HOURS" Junior doctors had been working on average 83 hours a week. Dr Martin Pattrick consultant physician, co-ordinating the scheme said: "We are very excited by this opportunity. On average Junior doctors spend 90 minutes a day on tasks which will be done by DAs. The hospital asked the regional health authority for the cash for the scheme. If it is a success, Junior doctors will be contracted to work fewer hours. The salary saving will go towards the DAs pay. A spokeswoman for the BMA praised the hospital as another step in the right direction for Junior doctors.

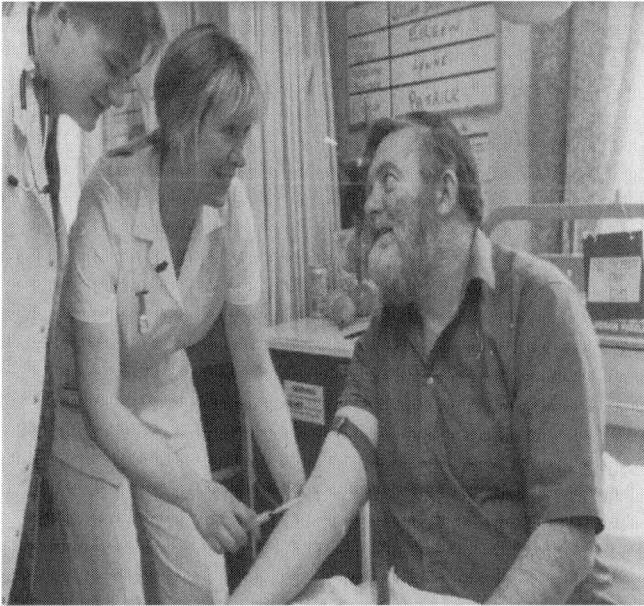

I had my picture taken with Dr Sean Kavanagh one of the first SHOs (senior house officer) we worked with. I love the way Bill was looking at me in the photo. He said I was nice and tall and so was he. Nurse management complained to Maureen for allowing the photograph to be published as we hadn't covered Bills name and I wasn't wearing gloves. You see management just like to make complaints; Bill was happy his name and photograph went in the paper. To be honest most people in the early days didn't wear gloves when taking blood and when we were taught gloves were not used.

In the photo you can see the cap is still on the needle.

The first practical task we learnt was how to take an ECG. We practiced on each other and learnt that one particular button gave a report of the reading. We were all OK, except for Sue whose ECG showed an abnormality. We approached Dr Randall the Senior Consultant in A&E to make sure she was OK. I liked Dr Randall and the way he greeted staff when he entered a ward. "Good Moaning All" he enjoyed Allo- Allo a classic TV show where the main character used the quote. He reviewed Sues ECG and reassured her everything was fine. I still have mine, normal sinus rhythm- normal ECG.

As soon as I was taught how to do something, I would be tested on Dr Hanleys ward round which told me he was asking about my training and was interested. He stayed up to date through the fifteen plus years I worked with him. Dr Hanley was always interested and I liked him for that. He scared me a little, sometimes quite a lot. He was a stereo typical male consultant of his day, looking down his nose through his glasses with an air of authority and power. He was well spoken wore a good suit and pointed shoes, left-handed with the most unusual hand writing. There was always a discussion with juniors and nurses if he dyed his hair or not as he had a good mop of black hair. I still don't know today if it was dyed. Course it must have been.

It took me a while to absolutely love working with him and understanding his ways. He worked really hard for his patients and didn't suffer fools at all, especially senior and middle management. His emails were famous, very cutting but always true. He hated post it notes because staff didn't use them properly, leaving them lying around with patient information on, not dated or signed. He collected them until he had a bag full, then would deliver them to the CEO. He was successful in having them banned from the hospital.

I have the greatest of respect for him and the way he treated patients and the junior doctors, who also had great regard for him. Clever man with entertaining conversational skills. I found his writing difficult to interpret, often others would ask me what he had written assuming because I worked with him, I could read his writing. It was my memory of his examination or discussion of the patient's plan that enabled me to decipher the words rather than reading his words. To be honest my writing deteriorated over the years too.

I had a problem with him once, and after getting advice followed by a quiet chat to him it was forgotten about and never mentioned again.

I'm pleased our working relationship continued, I learned so much from him. He had stories and you know I liked to listen to stories. I cannot tell them because they are not mine to tell but oil, rubber, feet and shoes, record player and cat come easily to mind. Dr Hanley became my husbands' doctor and we will be forever grateful for his expertise.

Taking blood was the next skill to be learnt. I can still see me and Sue in the outpatient patient department next to each other trying to bleed elderly patients. My first gentleman straight in no problem but I forgot to take the tourniquet off and there was blood all over his shirt. Sue later said she had never heard anyone be so apologetic. Taking blood is about repetition the more you do the better you get.

Our next skill was cannulation, inserting a needle covered by a plastic tube into a vein, removing the needle allowed intravenous fluids to be dripped into the plastic tube. I remember my first cannula, out on the ward with Oscar Minhas my new SHO. A chilled, clever and dry humoured man. When testing reflexes, he went about the task with such gusto, I named a rather large handled heavy tendon hammer after him (the Minhas). The cannula was needed for a patient on the high care unit as the nurses couldn't find a vein. What chance did I have, but that was my new role, a skill I needed to learn? I held the needle point for far too long next to the patients' skin and Oscar shouted down my ear "stick it in". I sort of jumped but in it went and bulls' eye first time. That was all I needed, my favourite job for a while until I was completely competent.

Oscar was one of the early SHO I worked with, I followed him around like a puppy, which I think he hated, I wanted to be in earshot of everything he said. I was learning every day in that role and it was the juniors that I worked with at the beginning that turned me into the efficient organised team member I became.

In those early days I remember being asked to do the ward round on my own and report back any findings. I was petrified, I can only imagine what the nurses were thinking at this point but we discussed the patient and I reported back. I believed the junior doctors were attending audits or training and yes one SHO was playing pool in the mess while I went round the patients alone. The SHO did another ward round that afternoon.

Taking blood cultures came next, basically it consisted of taking two bottles of blood and transferring the blood into two short fat bottles of liquid, a sort of broth and specific for what they call aerobic and anaerobic organisms. A positive blood culture means you have an infection in your bloodstream that can affect your entire body. You had to be particularly clean and precise when taking cultures as outside bacteria could ruin the samples. I quite liked taking blood cultures lots of needles and bottles. One day it went wrong, the blood didn't go in the bottle it shot into the air landing all over my head and uniform. I had to go home to shower and change and I remember thinking thank God I wore glasses and had my mouth shut.

Our training was of a good standard and to be honest once we had the practical tasks under our belt our learning came from the Junior doctors like Oscar, Leanne, Anti, Lulu, Ajay, Steve, Catherine and Claire. I was lucky to work with many excellent Junior doctors.

Improving our computer and administration skills at a local college we easily achieved NVQ level three in administration and later a European computer driving license (ECDL) qualification. My best memory of our first computer class was watching Jackie, use a mouse. She held it up to the screen and clicked away rather like a TV remote. Jackie asked so many questions we avoided sitting next to her.

We were a popular group with other Trusts and the idea of our hospital becoming a training centre for future DAs was being discussed. To check we were making a difference, I was shadowed to establish how much work I was taking off the juniors. These were the successful results. It wasn't just venepuncture and cannulation in the clinical red zone we performed ECGs and made decisions about which blood tests to take.

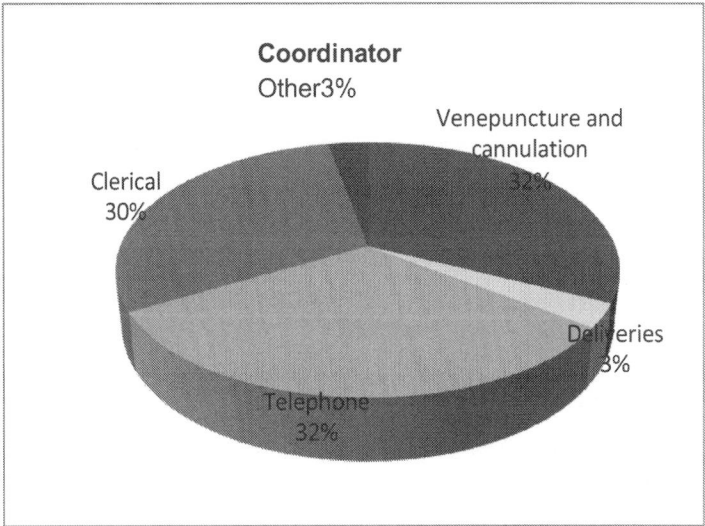

Coordinator

Other 3%

Venepuncture and cannulation 32%

Clerical 30%

Deliveries 3%

Telephone 32%

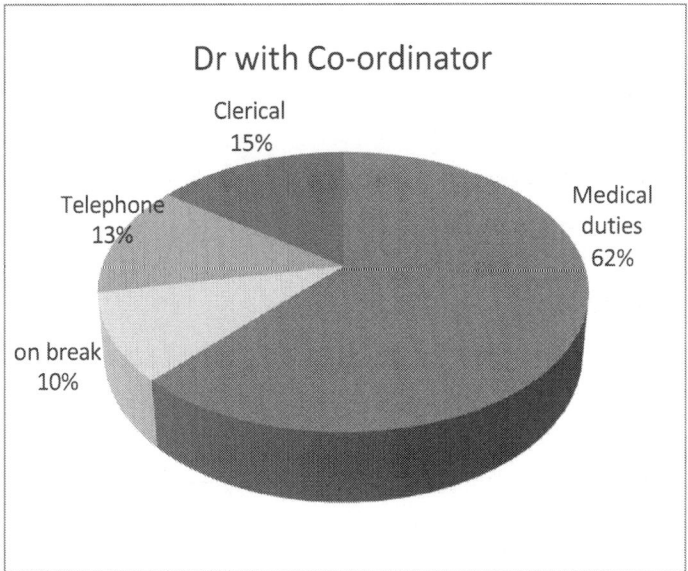

Dr with Co-ordinator

Clerical 15%

Telephone 13%

Medical duties 62%

on break 10%

Dr without co-ordinator

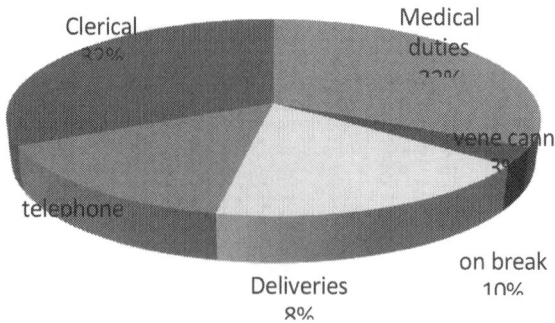

After shadowing and attended training, we were asked how we felt about joining the medical teams, which meant a change in working hours. We were given bleeps, mine was 4180. We were working on all medical wards the longest shift being on A&E. One of the DA's unwritten rules was never to deskill staff so taking blood or inserting cannulas were only performed when nurses bleeped the teams because they couldn't get access. If it became a doctors' job it became the DA's job.

The number of patients we saw depended on whether the teams were pre- or post-on call. If our team had been on call recently, forty patients could be on our list, if doctors were going on call in the next couple of days, our numbers would be much lower.

On the day before on call, when our patient numbers were at their lowest, one of the juniors always requested, to go for a coffee, at a particular time in the morning, she wanted to watch a cookery programme.

Hi Lulu.

Each morning a list was produced and printed, showing where patients were and which Consultant was responsible for their care. There were many discussions and disagreements over responsibility. It depended on the time the patient was admitted and the time they were first seen. The problem was the list, and particularly who input the data. To be honest, I'm not sure where inputting was done, the list was wrong more times than it was right. This was something that really got on my nerves, we were not talking about the responsibility for a car or a packet of biscuits, it was the care of a patient. Many times, I would seek out or call Dr Weir (Medical Lead) and ask him to see a particular patient, because the teams in the mess were arguing about responsibility. He was good at sorting juniors out, taking time to see the patient and documenting which consultant was responsible and giving that team a call.

We split the lists by consultant names and in the doctors mess you could hear the different teams comparing numbers "70 patients this week and we are on call tomorrow." That was because some consultants weren't as efficient at discharging as others.

I worked with very efficient teams so didn't have the luxury of looking after the same patients for long periods of time.

Every day new respiratory patients would be transferred to our team and with our discharges and on call we had a complete turnover of all our patients within a few days. Of course, we had very sick patients that stayed with us for longer periods but efficient teams get patients home as soon as possible, hospitals are dangerous places for catching infection and patients do so much better in their own environment when they are on the mend and ready to be discharged.

When the team were on call, DAs worked from A&E. We saw patients referred by local GPs. I started at 11am on these days and finished at 9pm. I loved working in A&E with its amazing staff, it was busy and I saw a variety of patients and conditions. My role, was to pick up the GP letter and take appropriate bloods, ensure the patient had an X-ray and ECG if required. I would find a bed for the patient if they needed admitting and write request cards for tests.

The patients were seen by doctors, so a history, diagnosis and plan could be documented and treatment started. I would check the patient had everything they required for transfer to the ward or for discharge. Just before the end of my shift I walked round the hospital, delivered request cards and informed the team in A&E of any empty beds I found on my journey.

The GP letters received by the RMO (registered medical officer) were in my opinion very poor. Some were a one liner. Others you could only go off the conversation between the GP and the doctor receiving the call, because you couldn't work out what was written on the referral. It was rare to receive a good letter and they were commented on by the teams, "well written referral", "who's the GP". The juniors knew the GP's that were good at providing the hospital with effective information compared to those that wrote two words.

Some activity in A&E I can recall and I have no idea why a particular event or patient stayed with me. One male from a local prison was escorted to A&E as he had been swallowing needles and inserting them under his skin, I can recall his X-Ray and the fact he was handcuffed. I didn't know his crime or ask.

Everyone was struggling to take blood from a patient who had been cutting his arms over a very long period and scar tissue was thick, making it difficult to feel or find a vein. I sat with him for a while listening to him talk about his anxiety. I did get his blood but will never forget the emotion of our chat.

My first cardiac arrest in A&E was dramatic, we were in resus when a patient arrested. Simon my first SHO asked me to squeeze the ambu bag which is a one-way valve and face mask, compressing the bag opens the valves forcing air through. Well, I was going hell for leather, much too fast and at the wrong pace, Simon started counting and I began to remember my training. The patient's oxygen levels were great though. Simon was a calm person and a nice SHO to learn from, he was another person I followed like a puppy.

Patients arrived in A&E complaining of the same thing. If one patient came in with COPD (chronic obstructive pulmonary disease) many others would, DVTs came in batches too. I wonder if any research has ever been done to establish how common this is. Just something I noticed.

When the hospital was full, I contacted other hospitals to arrange transfer for patients that needed admitting. This was never a popular thing to do, we would do our utmost to find a bed somewhere in the hospital, which is what created our outliers on surgical and gynaecology wards. Not the most suitable place for sick medical patients.

Ambulance technicians asked if I would help them learn to cannulate and take blood as they needed to perform a specific number of venepunctures before being signed off. This was the first time I was kind of teaching staff. How long had I been in the job, a few months, I had only just learnt myself but I was passing on anything I could.

One evening while on A&E I was bleeped by a colleague to enquire about her husband, he had attempted suicide after their recent break up. I found her husband and reassured her he was absolutely fine. Another colleague turned up in A&E after the death of her father she had taken an overdose. We chatted for a while and I thought how lucky she was to have enjoyed such an amazing relationship with her father.

A&E could be very exciting, but sad and often exhausting and stressful. It takes a particularly strong person to work in that department. The public can be ruthless in their comments and aggression was often witnessed. My memory of a female doctor being slammed against the wall stayed with me. She had an egg-shaped lump on her head for a long time after that attack.

A male was admitted with a stab wound and a gang of youths followed him into the department to finish the job. Security and police were always around.

Nowadays I think everyone wears alarms and the Police are stationed in the department. I hope staff working there feel safe. How very sad that we have come to this as a society. Hospitals should be a place of safety for all and anyone using the service should be respectful and appreciate the skills and dedication of the teams working there.

Some busy periods in A&E were predictable, snow and ice equals broken bones. Extreme weather conditions brought in patients with breathing difficulties. Providing sufficient staff was always a problem. Our governments over the years have stripped the NHS and specifically A&E because of their decisions to put pressure on Trusts to make savings they cannot afford. Governments failed to invest sufficiently to maintain adequate staff and resources to match the ever-increasing demand. Today is no different from 1994 in A&E; inappropriate patients turn up to be treated.

Working there was a fantastic learning curve for me, I witnessed the organisational chaos and how detached some doctors and nurses had become emotionally, walking in and out of rooms barely registering the human suffering they were seeing every day. I believe it is to protect their sanity as the suffering can be tangible at times. They are the team that witness all life experience, everyone at some point in their life will attend an A&E department and witness how precarious life can be with the tide of patients that flow into it.

The people arriving are often critical or in an apprehensive state, the teams there react quickly to the never-ending barrage of random injuries and perilous situations people find themselves in. It takes a very special person to spend their life working in an A&E department, such amazing staff.

My confidence began to grow and I thoroughly enjoyed my new role, it was so varied. Now there are bed managers, and medical assessment units that do the work the DAs performed in A&E and most patients are admitted straight to that unit and avoid A&E altogether. I never really understood this, I remember saying we need to speed up the discharge process at the end of the patients' journey rather than open more admitting areas, to me it was just another ward. Now I realise it was to help with targets, if the patient isn't in A&E, they cannot breach but as I said earlier diverting the flow of patients from A&E will not reduce the numbers in a hospital and it won't change the demand on the resources, but these medical and surgical areas keep opening. The hospitals will keep changing processes to meet Governments targets.

We were working more sociable hours now that our patients were directed to the medical assessment unit. Enjoying the camaraderie on the wards was back, we were spending more time on the medical wards with the nurses and clerks, building new relationships every day. Those nurses were hard working and I was beginning to feel part of their team too. Although I spent my time with the Junior doctors, we were always on one of the medical wards.

The main impact of the DAs role was on the Junior doctors, however, there was a significant positive impact for patients, ward staff and members of the multi-disciplinary teams. I think this was due to continuity. When the team needed urgent tests or procedures, the DAs had built up working relationships within all departments and that to me was the greatest impact this role had. We spent days observing in the labs, radiology, coding, medical records, the library and generally witnessing all hospital activity. As a group we met regularly during lunch and discussed our role. We knew it would evolve and sharing our experiences became an essential part of our learning. We had note pads full of information about blood tests and things useful to us, we called them our brains.

After a while I realised working with one medical team wasn't enough for me and I approached Maureen to discuss joining an extra team. She gave me the Ok, with advice to stick to the same specialty, I joined Dr David Weirs respiratory team.
Dr Weir was very different from Dr Hanley; he wasn't as sure or confident about the new role and it was quite obvious to me at the beginning. It was the little things he said that gave me doubts. "That's a doctor's job" was one thing he said. I wanted to say I know, but I'm trying to free up their time for other more important work" but I didn't. I was happy to continue and my thoughts were, I would eventually win him over. He was responsible for my work and I understood his hesitance.

Dr Weir was the silver fox of the Consultants, not quite as tall as me I'm 5'11", he always dressed well with sharp shirts and sleeves rolled up. I remember him not being allowed to wear shorts one hot summer as his wife didn't think shorts looked professional, I agreed with her. His humour was very dry, and ward staff didn't quite get him. I can honestly say I saw empathy in this man every time we did a ward round. He was caring and that showed. Dr Weir was OK, I liked the way he worked and yes, I think I won him over as he did support the role in the end. I found him approachable and although I didn't have many work problems, I would have been happy to go to him for advice. He occasionally mentioned his family although he was very private, little gems would slip out and I liked that. I have good memories of Dr Weir sitting listening to patients, on one occasion we approached a male alcoholic, Dr Weir asked "what can I do to help you". The patient responded with "I want to be able to walk like you" the patient had a very poor gait due to his alcohol intake. Dr Weir sat and chatted for a while, not judgemental, nice. He was also excellent at giving bad news this is a skill not all doctors have. Finding a private place to talk to a patient was almost impossible on the wards, Dr Weir would crouch very close to the patient and always discussed what they knew and wanted to know before he really said anything.

After a little reorganisation the other DAs began working with two teams. We also provided cover at weekends and bank holidays for post take ward rounds.

Very early on Saturday 15 June 1996, I was doing a post take round with one of the consultants, I think it was Dr Klass. These weekend rounds were usually quick as the consultants had seen most of the patients from the take the evening before. I never minded going in for a couple of hours on a weekend as my mother-in-law would look after the children. I walked to work and was going to take a taxi home that day, the taxi driver told me there was a bomb scare in Manchester and the streets were deserted and quiet.

A bomb scare/threat wasn't new, we had them regularly in Manchester and the shops had often been the target for the IRA who were the usual suspects for any threat. I didn't give it another thought got home and began to do some house work. I started with cleaning the outside of the house, mopping the step and cleaning the windows it was about 11.20. I noticed my windows melting as though they were running like fluid, then an incredible mighty boom which was followed by silence.

A bomb had detonated at the corner of Corporation Street and Cannon Street, it was the largest bomb detonated in Britain since the second world war. We lived about one and a half miles from the centre of town and I watched with my neighbours the resulting mushroom cloud over the city, dwarfing all the buildings even though we were on higher ground the mushroom was the eeriest thing I have ever seen. More than 200 people were injured with no fatalities. 700 million pounds worth of damage. The IRA warning gave time to evacuate 75,000 people from the area.

I received a couple of phone calls at home from Junior doctors who were working overseas checking on the impact of the bomb and I remember sending the Manchester Evening News over to Australia for them to see the devastation.

Within two years of working with the medical teams my confidence was building and Dr Pattrick asking Pat and me to teach 5th year medical students, how to take blood. We thought there would be a couple of students waiting for us in the undergraduate centre that first day, there were eighteen, all of them went quiet as we entered the room. We didn't have enough equipment and asked the students to be patient while we collected resources, we ransacked every medical ward in the hospital for stock.

We did OK, I took blood and cannulated Pat while the students watched. The next step was always a bit nerve racking the students split into groups, I supervised one group and Pat the other. We agreed they could only practice on a student if they allowed a student to practice on them. We felt that was fair.

I have great memories of medical students being enthusiastic and impatient. One student not waiting to be supervised or talked through the procedure put the tourniquet on another student and stuck the needle straight in, no preparation or equipment or bottle on the end of the needle. I remember Pat saying "what are you going to do now? You're on a ward and on your own, there is no one around to pass you anything what are you going to say to the patient"? He apologised but not before pulling the needle out without taking off the tourniquet or having gauze ready to press on the site.

Pat had to trust me taking blood and cannulating her as she had to observe the students as on one occasion a male student fainted, luckily it wasn't our first session and we were prepared for all eventualities, that we could think of anyway.

Dr Pattrick informed us our teaching sessions were going to be regular and supported us through college, with endowment funds. He paid our college fees and bought artificial arms for use during our teaching sessions. They weren't great but did the trick and we were glad to have no more fainting students. I remember our tutor being really impressed with the practical sessions we provided. The course took two years and we qualified in July 2000 achieving a further and adult education teacher's qualification and an IPD Assessor and verifier for staff taking

NVQs.

The undergraduate centre was an excellent place to teach, with good resources. Bernadette ran the department and supported our teaching sessions and we appreciated that. After a few years the undergraduate centre employed a clinical skills tutor who taught venepuncture and cannulation amongst other topics, Pat and I were redundant from training the medical students. We heard of her appointment through the usual grape vine, we should have heard through the deanery. We didn't even receive a thank you, very common in the NHS. Once the new tutor was working, she came to see us, the grapevine was much faster. Teaching the medical students gave me experience and confidence to teach other subjects.

There were many really good training sessions and courses provided by the Trust and I was very lucky to be allowed to access them. This role allowed time for training and development unlike the nurses who found it very difficult to access due to availability, ward cover and funding. Most in-house courses the DAs attended were for senior nurses and Junior doctors. We were never afraid to offer our opinion or ask questions. We ended up with a bit of a reputation. At first it was "Oh no you have the DAs in your group". Eventually that changed to "Oh good you have the DAs in your session they will keep things moving and interesting".

I socialised regularly with the junior doctors and members of the DAs group. I have good memories of one evening at Ann's house for a murder mystery dinner. Reading the cards and playing the game became more difficult as the wine flowed and the eyes blurred. We had to dress to suit our characters. Funniest for me was Ann, she kept in character all evening.

Ann and Lin from the ID wards

Sue, me, Pat and Jackie

Me and Sue always laughing

How lucky was I working with lovely SHOs.

Steve Fowler always smiling, he is sitting next to Rosie at the wall. I'm sitting next to the handsome Ajay Shetty; I remember he liked watches and wore them loose on his wrist.

I prepared and attended medical ward rounds every day, they are part of clinical activity and critical to the safe care of patients. To ensure a medical ward round is successful you have to prepare and that is where the DA's came in. We checked most information discussed on ward rounds from the notes to recent results, all charts, prescriptions and fluid balance. The DA's knew where each patient was up to in preparation for discharge. All radiology and agreed tests results were chased.

A good ward round improves the patients care and experience, it improves the satisfaction and training for the Junior doctors and the Consultants are always keen on improving the patient flow through and out of the hospital. The preparation and structure of a round was important so all patients received the correct amount of time needed to review and plan their care.

Generally, the teams would meet at 9am in the doctors' mess. There would be an SHO a HO and me. I started much earlier to establish where our patients were in the hospital and how many patients there were. Before nine I visited most wards to check our patient status and on a number of occasions, I entered a ward to find a person asleep behind a door, yes, lay on the floor with a pillow and blankets preventing anyone from entering the room. I know that night staff sleep on their breaks and they usually find a suitable area for all staff to have a nap while on break. Those behind the office door at 7am were not on a break, that was obvious by the way they responded to me entering the room. Full of apologises and an explanation why they were sleeping at that time of day.

Our meeting in the doctors' mess was to prioritise poorly patients, followed by anyone going home from medical wards, enabling the transfer of outliers, allowing elective surgical patients to be admitted. That was always the idea, but the ward round had a rhythm and after seeing the poorly patients we started on one ward and worked our way through the hospital. Members of the team dropped off, to complete take out drugs (TTOs) for the patients being discharged. Often, we would get to a ward and be unable to access our patients' notes as the notes trolley was being used by another team. We spent the day seeing patients and family members, ensuring there was a good plan to follow in every set of notes.

Prior to the ward round and before we had X-Rays on computer screens, I would collect old films for the team to compare the new films against the old images. X-Rays are very heavy and putting them in date order was an awful job. I remember consultants asking juniors what the foreign body was showing on films. It was usually a button, the internal workings of a lighter and the occasional bra wire. With one team the bra wire created a quiz, guess the cup size discussion with the male doctors, as if I wasn't there. No comment.

Many patients had their memory tested on the ward round. What day is it? What month is it? What is the name of the current monarch? etc. My best memory was of a nurse calling the answers from the opposite side of the curtain. I have no idea why she did this; she must have realised what we were doing. We laughed her answers were wrong the patient had a much better memory and knowledge.

Patients can be very inappropriate to doctors, I have witnessed them farting while being examined, burping in doctors faces and one old lady grabbed a young male HO and gave him a full-on kiss on the lips holding him by the cheeks with both hands. I hope he got over that one.

I recognised patients that had been treated at the hospital previously but under a different name. A female patient was admitted with Korsakoff syndrome a memory disorder caused by a severe deficiency of vitamin B1. Often from alcohol misuse, the condition was preventing her from remembering being mistreated by her partner the reason she was admitted. I was shocked and very sad by her situation. The consultant worked hard to ensure she had a place of safety when leaving the hospital, nice one Dr Weir.

I always tried to guess a diagnosis and as time went by, I became better at it. The condition I never got my head round was Munchausen syndrome a mental illness associated with severe emotional difficulties and needed help from another specialty. I was learning all the time in this role.

During the ward round the consultant or most senior member of the team would ask for specific tests or diagnostics to be performed and it was part of my role to ensure that these jobs were requested and documented as being ordered. One part of my role which was never really discussed or documented, remained one of the most important aspects and it happened after a ward round. The patient would call me over and ask, "what did the doctor say".

One of the most common training programmes in any hospital will be effective communication, having time to truly listen to your patient and their story and what matters to them is very important. For a patient there are many external distractions on a ward round, lots of noise, people talking and telephones ringing as well as their thoughts and worries whirring round in their head all taking them away from the information being relayed. The teams learned to shut these noises out, but the patients haven't, focusing can be very difficult. I would repeat what the doctors had said and ask the patients to explain to me what was happening next. This took time and that was something I was always ready to give.

While on the ward I was often asked by a family member if they could speak to the doctors. The doctors did their best to meet with family and I have a couple of memories that jump to mind. One family were not specific in who they wanted to speak to and the most Junior doctor offered and asked if I would go with him. The family were waiting in a room at the back of the ward. There were three family members and when the doctor entered the room they stood up. "Please sit down", but what he didn't do was sit himself. He hovered over them, looking down. I remember pushing a chair into the back of his legs to get him to sit.

Another large family kept asking for updates and the Junior doctor did his utmost every day with about three different members of the family. They were in dispute with each other and wouldn't nominate one person for the team to speak to. Why did the family involve the team in their family feuds, terrible when a family member is sick? In the end, the Consultant took control and the numerous daily updates stopped, I have no idea what was said.

Early on Wednesday mornings, patients would be rousing from sleep. On more than one occasion I would be on my own with the consultant and can honestly say no matter who was there the consultant rounds were as thorough. Again, on more than one occasion we would go to a patient and they would be wet, head to toe with urine. Urine dripping from sheets and pooling onto the floor. This really concerned us and we knew there was no one available to help. I don't think these were lazy nurses, they seemed busy no matter what time of day or night you were there. It was the admitting ward from your GP, a so-called short stay medical assessment unit, there never seemed to be enough staff to deal with all the patients' needs. Dr Hanley would look at me and I would say "don't, it will make me cry". He would say "go on then". I would get a bowl of water, clean sheets and night wear, we would wash and dress the patient and make the bed before his examination took place. Nice one Dr Hanley. Why the patients hadn't been checked regularly, I have no idea but the staff were made aware every time this happened but it continued.

Many patients were acutely unwell and their respiratory condition was usually just one of their problems. Most patients suffered from a wide range of disorders and had many obstacles affecting their day-to-day activity, including limiting their mobility. Mostly I remember patients being in bed rather than sat on a chair.

I took blood from TV celebrities and was present during the cardioversion of a comedian who was suffering with atrial fibrillation. The treatment involved giving his heart a controlled electric shock to restore a normal rhythm. We tried on his front and that failed, we turned him onto his side and gave him a shock front to back, it took several tries before his rhythm changed.

Some of my best memories were on Dr Hanley's ward rounds, like watching him taking photographs of sinks as they were in the wrong place, he took a lot of photos to make his point. I remember him standing on a window sill right above a patient. He was trying to repair the blinds to give the patient privacy. He passed me his phone and asked me to take his picture.

It was a privilege to be part of the ward rounds and listening to the teams discuss a patient's diagnosis and care was something I often didn't feel good enough for, the doctors were all so knowledgeable. I wanted the best for the patient and the two teams I worked with in my opinion were the very best.

The nurses rarely joined the ward round and I often completed a ward round book to update them on the information I had gained. I thought it was sad that nurses didn't join the round if only to listen to what was being said, you learn so much from just listening. They were always too busy and that is very sad.

A NEW HOME AND ANOTHER DIAGNOSIS

In 1996 looking for a new home became a priority and we found a house in Prestwich, North of Manchester. A proper money pit but loved the area. We had a canary yellow bathroom suite, a Cortina coloured 1950s pale blue and chrome cooker with two working burners, for the first few years. It didn't take long, only twenty years to sort the house out. I don't think it will ever be finished but we have loved living here.

I remember our first Christmas fifteen for dinner, two rings on the cooker and garden furniture in the dining room, what a fabulous day. I remember Dad spilling red wine all over the white table cloth and Jenny my eldest taking most guests to the pub while the dinner cooked. Dad looked well but by 2000 he was diagnosed with Motor Neuron disease (MND).

We had planned a large family holiday for the summer, but knew dad wouldn't be here to enjoy the trip, the deterioration soon became visible.

My sister Helen and I took dad to Malta and on the flight over the stewardess said he was lucky to have caring daughters, I didn't think he was lucky a fit cyclist getting MND. I remember Helen asking me who took control of money when on holiday. Vin always did the money for us, too much effort for me. Helens husband Nick did the same. God this is going to be good, we sat there making a chart on a piece of card how much a pound, a fiver and tenner was in Maltese Lira. It was a weird time, Helen, dad and me sharing a hotel room.

Dad was peg fed at night through a tube in his stomach (percutaneous endoscopic gastrostomy) the liquid dripped slowly in over the night, the room hummed with the sound of the pump. On a couple of occasions, dad turned the pump off and didn't bother with his food. He couldn't speak or eat and holding his head up was now difficult and his chin would slip under the rigid neck brace he wore.

During the holiday we did a little sightseeing in the day and ate out most evenings, poor dad just sat and watched me and Helen eat, that must have been awful. Dad spent most of the holiday being pushed around in a wheelchair and occasionally he would get out and walk a short distance pushing the chair himself. He was very weak. We would meander back to the hotel after our evening meal and occasionally watch the hotel entertainment, usually ball room

140

dancing.

One evening dad asked for a rum and black and had to syringe the rum into the peg himself, just in case. Helen wanted to know why blackcurrant in the rum, laughing I said "so he can taste it when he vomits." Helen and I have precious memories from that week, watching dads face as I tried to direct her, reversing a car, he was so frustrated and we just laughed. Poor dad.

Many guests in the hotel had disabilities, a proper busman's holiday for me. Carers trying to maintain some sort of normality in their lives. One afternoon we laughed that much Helen and I had to leave the lounge area, we had been listening to new guests asking who picked this bloody hotel, looking round at the disabled bodies in the room.

Our carers, I am one, are undervalued in this society. Basically, all carers are on their own, groups, departments, GPs, hospitals and the NHS all say they support carers but they don't. Every carer requires diverse support at different times. Over a greater period, I have required someone to help me to wash and dress my husband at other times I needed help mixing and putting up his drips. The times I needed help with the gardening or decorating in fact all practical requirements of running a home and all activities of daily living.

Carers carry guilt, pegs on a washing line, for me one

peg represented the money I needed to earn to keep my family afloat. Another peg on the line was being able to afford a car to drive where I needed to be for work and for caring at home for family, so saving for me became a mission. I was spreading myself quite thinly and feeling guilty that I was failing in all aspect of my care duties/responsibilities whatever you want to call them.

Working out dad had MND wasn't easy, we all knew something wasn't quite right and eventually my sister (a specialist nurse) worked it out. This was an awful time, my mother-in-law had recently had a heart attack, ending in a triple bypass, another guilty peg. My mum was wheel chair bound with chronic rheumatoid arthritis; her main carer was my dad, another guilty peg. I just couldn't be there all the time.

My husband unwell with his lung condition and to be honest I have no idea how I managed to stay focused, but I did, I can be strong sometimes.

As I was saving for my car I would go to mums on the tram from work, Crumpsall to Stretford. I would get off in Manchester pop into M&S and buy goodies for them. Then jump back on the tram to finish the journey. Walk, it felt like miles my feet were so sore all the time.

Generally, mum and dad managed for themselves, there were carers going in, plus my sisters and brother visited regularly, lots of people popping in and out. Mum loved the goodies from M&S, chocolate covered ginger biscuits, blackcurrant and grape juice, individual portions of Victoria sponge, steak and pepper sauce, cooked chicken and anything with crab.

Mum called me at work to let me know dad received a machine to help him communicate. You know the kind, type your words and the weird electronic voice speaks. Typical, they left the machine in a female voice. He never used it properly.

Dad was a cyclist and continued until he couldn't hold his head up, we always thought he would die on his bike. There are different types of MND, dad had Bulbar which affects fewer people than Amyotrophic lateral sclerosis (ALS) the more common type. Bulbar affected the muscles in your face, throat and tongue, life expectancy is very short, between six months and a couple of years from first symptoms. Dad wasn't diagnosed straight away, once the diagnosis came, we knew there wasn't much time left. Dad couldn't speak or eat and looked very weak but walked into St Ann's hospice for a rest, well that's what we were told.

I remember every detail of this Thursday; I was preparing the ward round on H4 when an urge to ring the hospice became overwhelming: -

"How's my father Richard Rothwell".
"He's had a good night and is eating his breakfast".

"Can you take the phone to dad and tap it when you put the phone to his ear, then I will know to start speaking". "Certainly", I could hear footsteps and a tap.

"Hi dad its Moira I'm bringing mum to see you after my shift, hope you are resting well".

"Hello, hello".

"I'm sorry can you give the phone back to the nurse". "That isn't my father, my father cannot speak and he wouldn't have been eating breakfast". "I'm sorry; who did you say your father was". "Richard Rothwell".

I could hear footsteps again but the conversation was over.

I called straight back she hadn't told me anything about my dad.

"Hello"

"I spoke to a nurse a moment ago, however she hasn't told me anything about my father".

"I'm sorry, we are on the telephone to your mother, your father passed away this morning".

Dad died on June 21 aged 71. I put the phone down and rang Vin. I had been sitting next to Carl the respiratory nurse, he bleeped Jackie to let her know my sad news. I walked down the corridor to the doctors' mess with tears running down my face to be met by the DA's. I'm grateful they sat with me until Vin arrived. We collected Margaret one of my sisters and drove to mums.

I had a pact with Margaret, we wanted to tell each other when mum or dad died. I didn't really tell her dad had died, I just mentioned our pact and she began to cry knowing he had passed away.

When we arrived at the hospice the priest was pushing his way through our group who were going slowly because mum couldn't go any faster. He was saying he had an emergency, we all stood back to let him past, he hurried into dads' room. The nurse walking toward us looked a little stressed and asked for me, she began to apologise for the conversation earlier. It was fine, I understood and told her not to worry, we all make mistakes, I'm sure that nurse will pay more attention to the names of her patients in future.

I took a week off work and as a family we organised dads funeral and made care arrangements for mum. We started at St Anns church in Stretford then onto the crematorium at southern cemetery. We had one car and mum sat at the front next to the driver; it was easier to get her in and out, from that seat. Me and my siblings sat at the back. I have one memory sitting in that car, Helen my youngest sister asking "where's dad". Then the giggles kicked in.

After dad's death I changed my hours and began to work four days a week allowing me to spend time with mum every Friday. I didn't have to do much cleaning, occasionally vacuuming but always disinfecting the surfaces, mum had a manky cat. I think Margaret one of my sisters did most of the cleaning. I do remember doing her washing, every resident had a particular slot for washing and I think my mum took extra time on a Friday, I used the slot of another tenant, I never asked I just put the washing in. Marion the residential home manager told me off a couple of times.

Mum had joints removed from her feet due to arthritis, she was a size nine shoe and after the operation a size six/seven. She loved a good foot rub and a bit of pampering and most weeks that's what I did. I soaked her feet and tried to cut her horn like nails. Picking the dead skin out of her toes. Lovely, she used to laugh. Finally, I would rub in cream. I will never forget the feel of mums' legs though, they were like wood, the strangest thing.

Often my eldest daughter Jenny and grandson Harry would come with me to mums making the day extra special for her. We would take mum shopping in Stretford and occasionally have lunch in a café there. Mum loved eating out, which she missed since dad's illness and death.

I have good memories of our shopping trips and mum shouting at people. She couldn't see very well and was partially deaf, while going around Tesco she would hear other shoppers and would shout "are they talking to me". Occasionally she was quite rude. I apologised a few times for mum but would be laughing inside.

One morning she called to tell me her carers hadn't turned up and she had fallen out of bed, she couldn't reach the emergency cord. She was crying? "I'm on my way." I jumped in a taxi to Butler court in Stretford from my mother ship and found mum half in bed and half on the floor, she had been incontinent and was visibly upset. I gave her a cuddle and got her on the bed. It wasn't easy moving mum about she was always in pain, over the years she had new knees and hips, bones removed from her toes and her wrist bones filed down.

On numerous occasions when I entered mums flat, I thought she had died, her chair was facing the door at the entrance to her flat. She would be sat in her chair, her head to one side and her mouth dropped open. She looked pale and dead. She knew I thought this and when I woke her, she would laugh. Very funny mum. I spent most Fridays with her Jenny and Harry laughing and caring.

Visiting mum in Stretford

On Tuesday 11 September 2001 I was on the ward round with Andy Jones our respiratory registrar (definitely one of my favourites) and Orla a tall competent SHO, when news of the coordinated terrorist attacks by the Islamic terrorist group al-Qaeda was relayed to us. Orla went running to call her brother who worked in the area. I left Andy doing the ward round on his own and sat in a side room in shock watching the events unfold on a TV while a patient slept. I stayed in the side room for a short while, then re-joined Andy to finish the ward round. When that second plane hit the building, it was like watching a movie not the reality of the world we live in. I sat there in shock that humans can be so terrible to each other.

That evening my son and his girlfriend were going on holiday, flying from Manchester. When I eventually got home, they were packed and all excited for their first holiday together, they hadn't heard the news. We encouraged them to leave very early for their flight and remember saying it will be the safest one you will ever take, because of the security checks. We did worry that evening, he arrived safely and I was so grateful my prayers were answered.

Around the November of that year matron desperately needed staff for yet another winter pressure ward, and pleaded with me to work a nursing shift she couldn't cover. I agreed to work an early shift with two trained and one auxiliary nurse.

This was the only medical ward I worked on in a nursing capacity. I slotted back in without a problem but was shocked when I helped the first patient. He cried as I assisted him to wash and shave, he'd been a patient for three days and this was his first wash. I was absolutely furious. I realised the other staff were busy except one nurse sitting at the computer. I asked when she would be able to help the patients?

I gave her an hour then asked her for the bleep number of the on-call nurse manager, "What do you want that for"? Although I knew full well the number, I wanted her to know I was going to report her, which I did. She didn't seem concerned. I spent the whole shift washing and shaving patients, doing observations and emptying catheter bags, that was the last shift I ever worked in a nursing role on any ward.

Why had standards dropped or were standards always different on medical wards compared to surgical wards? I don't think so, I remember the first medical wards I visited every day as a new DA and the nurses were amazing, caring and supportive of their patients so what was wrong. Was there enough staff for a medical ward two trained plus two auxiliaries for an early shift? Maybe it should have been more, I don't have the answer, all I can say is one trained nurse spent all morning and I mean all morning sat at the computer. What she was looking at, I don't know, it wasn't prescriptions or patients notes, they were not electronic.

I witnessed many arrests over the years and with that how people manage in very stressful and emotional circumstances. I remember a couple of Junior doctors young and fit running down the corridor as their bleeps had informed them of an arrest on one of the wards. I was running faster than the juniors and shouted to them you won't be there first someone bleeped you to attend. Their fear of arriving first held them back. I remember many tears when patients hadn't survived especially if the patient was young.

Watching the junior's confidence grow and bloom within weeks or months was a joy to be part of. Occasionally a HO wouldn't settle and I witnessed a doctor leaving his chosen profession because of stress. A few times the consultants asked me to be extra supportive with a particular HO, to keep an eye on them. They weren't coping and witnessing this in such a young bright person was awful, we didn't manage to keep that one doctor very sad. I hope he found a career that made him happy.

One of the most traumatic arrests I ever witnessed happened during a ward round. The trauma for me wasn't the patient that arrested, it was the family's reaction to grief that traumatised me. The juniors were bleeped to an arrest on one of the wards. After about ten minutes me and Dr Weir followed them. As we opened the main doors to the ward the patient that arrested was on the left-hand side with the curtains pulled around the bed. There were no visible staff. I'm assuming they were all behind the curtain, but that would have been way too many people especially when the ward was kicking off. They were scared, and I don't blame them.

At the top of the ward a large male was head butting

the wall and wailing. The consultant David Weir was fantastic, he walked straight down the ward and took the man into the dayroom. I looked round and saw a female screaming trying to pull the curtains down from their rails. A couple of children were near the patient that had arrested. Visitors were obviously in shock and took sanctuary in the toilets at the end of the ward. I remember encouraging the woman and children into the office. That was the most aggressive response I ever witnessed to an arrest, to grief. The patient passed away and other family members began to arrive, many people have strong responses to grief, I will never forget that family.

So much changed in this job not just for the DAs but for the doctors too. At first Junior doctors inserted chest drains, performed ascetic taps, did lumbar punctures and bronchoscopies on the wards, they reviewed daily any patients the team had on the high dependency unit or Intensive and coronary care units. Every day was different, I loved that aspect of the role. Things moved on and those procedures and reviewing very sick patients on ICU and CCU were being done in specialty areas or theatres and by specific doctors.

When the juniors stopped performing these tests and reviewing critical patients, I felt they would be deskilled. During these procedures, I did the dirty nursing and remember the dramatic or difficult ones. If I became concerned, I went for help and would happily interrupt a meeting or ward round to get assistance for a patient and/or Junior doctor.

I asked one consultant to intervene when a junior had tried a number of times to do a lumbar puncture. I was always an advocate for the patient. By this stage I was happy to challenge most things.

One afternoon with a registrar (reg) we were on ICU which had been moved to an area off the theatre corridor due to renovations. The registrar needed to do a bronchoscopy, a procedure that allowed him to see inside the patient's airways. I was the dirty nurse preparing and opening the equipment. The bronchoscope is a thin tube with a camera on the end. It is passed into the patients' airways. I remember being asked to take the biopsy, which is really only opening and closing the handles of a pair of scissors and putting the contents into solution in a sample pot. The things the DA's did. Loved working with that reg and remember before the consultants' ward round, he would ask for suggestions to wind one particular consultant up. JFM always thought of something to create a debate.

There was one reg I was a little unsure of because of one experience. He was doing a central line; I was the dirty nurse and he struggled to get the line in. He kept telling the patient to keep still but the patient wasn't moving. It was his inability to insert the line and he lost his temper; I wasn't going to stand there and listen to the Reg speak to the patient in such a brusque manner. I told him the patient wasn't moving. The reg was also quite sweaty; I was concerned his sweat would drip onto the clean site. I cannot remember who did the central line in the end. That reg was a bad- tempered bugger, not my favourite. Thank God I only had one reg like that.

The way I viewed patients and staff was changing, I witnessed conversations and incidents that were challenging emotionally. Wards can be a very stressful place to work and witnessing the odd brusque doctor and the occasional tricky patient can be difficult, especially in an environment where communication could be poor. I can still hear the patient centred mantra, but to be honest patients found it difficult to speak to some doctors and nurses. How can patients be at the centre of their own care when they don't know what is available or on offer for their condition? They don't know who the best specialist is or what the best treatment is? We have to rely on teams giving patients the information they require. I was lucky I had proactive positive teams to learn from. I hope all teams were as thorough as very few patients questioned the professionals.

I witnessed genuine care and attention to detail where patients felt the kindness of the team treating them, the teams were interested and concerned. There was always a balance and for most of my time in the medical teams this positive statement was what I experienced.

One popular highly competent registrar appeared at times indifferent to patients', you could see his eyes glaze over. I told him on a couple of occasions, he had lost interest in what the patient was saying. I knew he cared, he must have had other things on his mind but if I noticed, patients would notice too.

Doctors are human and suffer from the same problems and stresses we all do, they deal with their own problems and sometimes become disheartened witnessing situations and dealing with management that shifts so much and quickly, revealing crisis after crisis. They witness daily the lack of nurses affecting the very meaning of care.

Like all of us maintaining concentration can be difficult if you are suffering from anxiety or dealing with personal problems. That was where the teams supported each other, once any of the doctors were alerted to a junior experiencing difficulties someone would step in and support them.

I'm just thinking of the teams and I don't mean just the two I worked for but all of them, the DAs and junior doctors could ask any SHO for support, and we did especially in times of annual leave, training or sickness.

When it came to inserting intravenous cannulas, I was good, it was rare I couldn't insert one. Occasionally I would be bleeped by other teams struggling.

The next step for a critical patient without IV access was a central line in the internal jugular or femoral vein. When I struggled, I couldn't ask the junior doctors or nurses because it was them that struggled in the first place. I knew if I contacted the Registrar, they would do their utmost to site the cannula because if they couldn't they would have to do the central line themselves. There was always backup you just had to know who to ask, and I loved that support.

Portraying the events in a chronological order has been difficult and some stories are out of kilter but that doesn't matter. Some of the juniors like patients stuck in my mind for some weird or funny reason.

Helen was one of these. She had blonde hair sometimes dyed red sometimes spikey, a whirling dervish, she was always on the go, never sitting still, not for a moment. There is a stick with a woodpecker that goes up and down pecking at the stick in a frantic manner, that was Helen, loved this junior. She was thorough and exceptionally conscientious and I often thought if I was the headachy type I would have a permanent headache working with her. I have two good memories of Helen one her wedding preparation and the wedding to the ID registrar Sa Khoo. This was the first wedding I attended of one of the juniors, a couple of us went to the church in Liverpool then a group of us went by coach to the evening reception, I sat with Leanne on the coach journey, I just remember laughing.

My other memory of Helen and her total commitment to patients happened when we were short of Junior doctors, she was working nights. I was asked to do the ward round on my own, document changes in blood results, problems voiced by patients or nurses and document any results I chased. WOW, I was so nervous. The fear of missing something helped me triple check everything that I was doing. I remember going on my first ward, the staff nurse and ward clerk that day were so helpful. I made my list and meet Helen after she had slept to make a plan. It was around two pm when we met up in the doctors' mess, over coffee.

We discussed every patient on our list and Helen added her comments. I then went back to the patients and followed her instructions and documented in the patients notes. I sought SHOs or HOs like Leanne to sign prescriptions and ask further advice. This went on for five days, patients were seen by consultants and registrars on their ward rounds, all the work was checked. I was a band three. Thank God for the amazing junior doctors and nurses that helped me that week.

Jackie, Leanne and me listening to jazz
at
Helens wedding

I met Leanne recently in 2024, she is now a grown-up doctor a consultant and Head of Department in Infectious Diseases at the mother ship. She looks and sounds just the same and I really appreciated her looking after my husband. Again, how lucky am I to have worked with such wonderful people. If she is your doctor, lucky you.

Twice a year we would get different juniors joining our team, either a HO or SHO. It was so nice working with young people and watching their confidence grow. One new HO arrived and the child in me took over, he was called Dr Dick and I smiled every time I introduced him to the ward staff. I had quite a few childish moments with names and silly things that happened but laughter was my thing and I tried to be light hearted but not always successful.

THE CHALLENGE

Our line managers changed a lot over the years. I remember those managers that ignored emails sent from DAs, managers that never updated the group, those with no time for us because we had no influence. However, we did have a couple that I appreciated, my favourite was Mary Livesey a softly spoken heavy smoker. She was the most proactive with our group and was looking to introduce a lead position, a person who would take over training and line management. Mary wasn't full of bull shit like some of the other managers we met. I can still see her telling me, if you can manage the DA's, you can manage anyone, they are a tough group to manage. I already knew that. She called me up to her office for a chat one day and asked me if I would apply for the position, saying she would support me if I took the job. I did and she did support me. I received a pay increase to a band 4. Mary sent me on courses to gain management and leadership qualifications to support my development and to prepare me for what she called THE CHALLENGE.

I spent a couple of afternoons a week in classroom setting gaining my first management and leadership qualifications. I was loving the training which spurred me on to want more. I worked my way through training using the group as evidence of success. Thanks ladies.

Our numbers were increasing and over the years we were joined by Lin, Sylvia, Alison, Lisa, Mike, Joanne, Libby, Heather and Suzanne, all joining us at different times. Sylvia was a trained nurse and I thought would be the natural person to take over when I moved on, as that was my intention, I never intended to stay so long.

My mission was to change the job title and get the DA's a pay review. I realised it didn't take much to change a job title and after a brief discussion with senior teams we became doctors' associates (DAs). It did change again years later but I cannot remember when or what they are called now. My preference was always medical team co-ordinator it was a good description for the role.

Supervising the DAs wasn't easy as Mary predicted, they created a problem at every opportunity and would often be found at the union office. I would get a bleep telling me "They have been here again", it became a running theme for a while, a reaction to being managed.

Mary was great, we used to laugh at the time they spent moaning about me, but that was OK it was a response they needed to work out. I believe in the end they realised I was on their side and spent most of my time trying to increase their salary and defending the role to the sceptics.

The DAs were working with specialty teams and providing cover or supporting other teams with no Junior doctors. We had a rota working with the on-call consultants over holiday periods, Easter and Christmas. This way we experienced working with a variety of specialties.

I occasionally saw concern from Junior doctors with the plan of care written in a patient's notes. Most if not all juniors found it difficult to challenge their seniors because they needed a reference and were regularly assessed by the Consultants. That was another skill the DA had, knowing who to contact for help. Numerous times I asked a Senior House Officer or Registrar from my team to help support a junior from another team because they weren't happy with the plan of care for a particular patient. They would review the patient and amend the plan. This was how doctors saved face.

More transparency was needed with open discussion within the hospital to learn from each other, we are all human, all learning and all make mistakes.

I can honestly say the Consultants I worked with were exceptional and I don't remember ever a conversation challenging their plan of care. One sort of challenge I remember when a doctor prescribed bananas for a patient with a low potassium. I recall the conversation with another team trying to work out how many bananas the patient should eat to build the potassium level. It's all well and good taking the piss out of a senior, but if you don't put them right how will they learn.

Big gripe for me on a couple of wards, you couldn't log onto the ward computer especially first thing in the morning. Games had been played and staff never logged out which caused a delay for me getting results. Often, the computers had been turned off and they took an age to boot up. There were many reasons why we were unable to access systems and there were problems most days. Luckily some consultants and many Junior doctors were computer enthusiasts and would sort out the problem, avoiding a long telephone queue for the IT department, everyday most wards were in that telephone queue.

Some daft things I remember: -

Many of the doctors I met were left-handed and the females wrote much neater than the males. One junior drank pints of milk every day. The cleaner in the mess always saved dry bread for one junior doctor he liked dry toast "to keep his energy up".

When a patient dies and the family choose cremation the Junior doctors complete a form for which they receive a fee. Many donated their fees to charity. One junior was very upset after the death of a patient and I remember attending a patients' funeral with her.

Locums were used at the hospital for many different reasons, covering sick leave or large workloads, they cover gaps in service or rotas due to retention and recruitment problems. Not all locums are the same, I remember conversations of concern about a couple of locums and the juniors speaking to the medical director to prevent them being employed at the Trust again. This frightened me, thinking that they may have the qualification but how did they get them, and why do they still have them.

One female doctors' attempt to catheterise a patient stayed with me, the patient refused point blank to open her legs for the catheter to be inserted. I remember being shocked at the questions the doctor asked her, on the lines of abuse. That poor lady looked terrified by the probing questions the junior asked. The consultant wasn't impressed.

One male junior made me a hot honey and lemon drink in the doctors' residence when I was full of a cold. He also visited me at home one Saturday.

I was looking out of the bedroom window and noticed him walking along the reservoir opposite my house. He had to climb the fence to come in for coffee.

One weekend at lunch I sat listening to a couple of Junior doctors playing their musical instruments. They entertained me for an hour. How nice is that. We had many nights out and I remember one summer ball where four of the Junior doctors played as a band, they were really good.

Some patients were really special and you never knew which one would get to you. I often saw juniors bringing things in for patients, soap, toothpaste and sweets little thing that made their day. One lady I remember asked for a boiled egg and brown bread and butter, the canteen and patients' kitchen didn't do boiled eggs. A couple of times a week she received a boiled egg with brown bread.

One day while walking along the corridor with a female SHO and HO one of the consultants made a comment that we looked like amazons. I really liked that comment and have used it regularly since. Three tall women together, not something I see every day.

Amazons were a tribe of warrior women believed to live in Asia Minor, the daughters of Ares and Harmonia. When I'm with my daughters and granddaughters I always describe us as Amazons now.

Every Wednesday lunch time a grand round for medical staff and local GPs took place. At this event, lunch was provided, followed by a presentation and discussion of patients' conditions and treatments. The room held about eighty people and I would often go with juniors who were presenting. This was a fantastic opportunity for doctors to discuss their plans of care and outcomes, highlighting anything that retrospectively they could have done better. Many of these presentations went right over my head but on the whole, I learned something new every time including, how many people with full stomachs go to sleep when the lights go out. This often happened and I would nudge anyone next to me that began to snore. However, I remember everyone creeping out quietly one Wednesday leaving a couple of snoring sleeping doctors and my consultant was one of them. Jackie was best out of our group for closing her eyes after lunch, but never got to the snoring stage.

The Drs Mess became a pet project for Pat one of the DAs, she was exceptional at organising and making improvements. When we arrived, the mess received coffee, tea, sugar and a couple of packets of biscuits, plus daily newspapers.

By the time Pat finished there were coffee machines, new furniture, lots of goodies and good coffee from Makro plus plenty of bread and spreads for making toast. The store cupboards were full and that mess was probably the best in Manchester. Well, done Pat.

Smoking cessation was high on the agenda for all Trusts. One consultant asked Sue and me to run smoking cessation clinics in the cardiorespiratory department. We would collect data from each session to produce information that would if I remember correctly, support employing a smoking counsellor in the respiratory clinics. We were happy to help, I found it quite amusing, Sue still smoked and the consultant, I hesitate to say, smoked on nights out. Anyway, we held our clinics on different days in a lovely setting in the cardiorespiratory department. We asked a specific list of questions and added further information after each appointment. We took carbon monoxide (CO) levels and used the results as a motivational tool. The CO is usually undetectable around 24 hours after a last cigarette. I remember patients lied about their last cigarette, "I haven't had one in weeks", and their CO reading were always high. One marijuana smoker had CO levels through the roof and his response was "I better get baking then".

No comment.

Mainly it was about having the right conversation and boosting motivation. We wrote prescriptions for nicotine replacement therapy. The prescription pads had all been pre signed.

My role was changing and with a new manager Jude my pay was reviewed. I was promoted to a band five and spent my time juggling priorities between junior teams, shadowing and writing reports on different ways of working at other hospitals and departments. My favourite role was always with the junior doctors but I needed to move on.

The doctor's mess was a really good place for getting away from the stresses of the day. There was often someone there to talk to or just to sit quietly. However, a certain group of doctors during cricket season would spend far too much time there watching TV.

The Drs mess was a place for recuperation after a night out and the doctors had many, they worked and played hard. I have wonderful memories of the times I spent with them, lots of laughter and in my case drunken dancing. My son would pick me up at the end of the night. He was fantastic if I went into Manchester, he always picked me up "it's not safe mum". Good lad.

Occasionally I would be the one left holding up a junior doctor. I remember one tall female wrapped round a lamp post outside the Lass O' Gowrie pub in Manchester. She had been drinking white lightning cider, I know!! I had to carry her to the doctors' residence that evening. The conversation with switch board was memorable, "if she doesn't answer Keep bleeping her until she does". I bleeped her from home too, she was up and on call the next morning.

On one night out a colleague came to me for help a new senior doctor had passed out on the floor in the gents. We managed to get him to a seat, I don't know how he got home but I'm sure someone would have helped him. What was I the clean-up woman for drunken doctors? Probably, but I do remember them helping me unzip my trousers (side zip) one night when I had drunk too much. I remember standing in the ladies saying "if I cannot get these trousers down, I'm just going to pee right through them". One kind junior helped and unzipped my pants. Another supported me and Jackie one evening after too much wine, I have no idea how she managed it, but she did. God bless her.

Charlotte, one of the Juniors, mess treasurer at one point decided to clear the kitty as funds had built up.

She organised a subsidised hospital ball and a night out in Manchester. She carried a money belt that evening, I thought it was a bit dangerous. Thanks Charlotte. Another evening, I remember sneaking into the side door of the Ritz with the juniors. Good times. Lots of dancing with Anti and Catherine, loved these ladies. Chatting to Leanne and watching her drinking pints with Dr Weir who wasn't really drinking (he pretended to down a pint).

Steve Fowler made me smile, Simon, James, Aurellia, just a few more doctors' names that come easily to mind. Thanks, you were amazing company, I probably liked and respected you so much for the way you were with patients too.

Two SHOs Ajay Shetty and Claire Barker helped me celebrate my 40th birthday at a large family party. They bought me a beautiful brooch which I still wear today. Thanks.

Claire Barker my snow white of the juniors, had dark bobbed hair and pale skin, she always wore red lipstick. She was my confidant, I could tell her anything, a clever caring lady.

One Christmas, the chest/respiratory night out was at a Chinese restaurant in the centre of Manchester.

The usual suspects were there respiratory and cardiology consultants, Junior doctors, secretaries, nurses, cardiorespiratory and CCU staff. Talk about too much drinking, one member of the cardiorespiratory team took her top off at some point, and vomited on the table. How embarrassing, I sat in the taxi holding a black plastic bag around her neck. The driver was adamant if any vomit lands in the taxi, he was going to fine us. Even better, guess who got a mouth full off her daughter for letting her mother get in that state. I didn't even get a thank you for that one.

Occasionally I witnessed the recovery of Junior doctors with a drip being used to rehydrate them after drinking too much. No comment.

On many occasions I witnessed tears from the juniors trying to prevent the inevitable from happening to patients.

I just loved the people I worked with in this role and I'm so grateful to have met them in their junior years. I bet they are still amazing caring people.

THE TEARS BEGAN

Vin, my husband had been under the care of Dr Hanley for a while now, he was the ideal consultant to deal with the questions Vin would ask in clinic. He wasn't like other patients he challenged everything the doctors said, always wanting proof for the safety and effectiveness of any kind of medication he was offered. I'm sure Dr Hanley had a job to convince him of anything.

Eventually after many years of discussion he tried steroids. He loved the high but hated the low which followed when the dose was reduced. Steroids gave him an appetite, and a feeling he could achieve so much more.

On his clinic visits Vin often met the registrars I worked with. He knew the exceptional ones, those standing out against individuals that needed reassurance from the consultant. Jenny Hoyle and Andy Jones come easily to mind as being confident. Andy is now a professor; he was the doctor that originally referred Vin to Wythenshawe to see a physician called Dr Leonard.

That year Vin got shingles and was admitted onto one of the infectious diseases (ID) wards at the mother ship. I remember calling my son and asking him to bring bleach and cloths for me to clean the bathroom which smelt and looked terribly stained. This was the new part of the hospital; I was shocked to see the state of the bathroom. With Vin upstairs on the ID ward, I was doing the ward round with one of the juniors on H4. He was blaming me for something that I cannot remember, I'd had enough. I remember marching into Dr Weirs clinic crying, red faced and black eyed from mascara, telling him I was going home. Basically, I just couldn't cope and that was where it came out. Poor Dr Weir didn't know what to do with me. I visited Vin on the ward, went home and took a couple of days off.

During one of Vins outpatient appointments at Wythenshawe, Dr Leonard his physician mentioned a lung transplant. I didn't attend all Vins appointments there were so many, but that was one I'm sorry I missed. He was still working full time for a very famous company that had absolutely no systems in place to support sick staff.

Vin was getting increasingly short of breath and after attending clinic he returned home with a pulse oximeter to measure the oxygen in his blood. Normal readings are between 95 and 100 this is known as oxygen saturation (sats). Vin was asked to record his sats while performing regular daily activity like getting out of bed and after a shower.

His readings ranged between 73 and 90. I was in melt down knowing what was coming. At the time, adverts on the TV showed a woman on home oxygen with tubing running around doors and along the floor, I knew that was our future.

He returned to clinic to be told he needed a transplant assessment. He was assessed for home oxygen the same day. I hadn't been in clinic with him, due to some stupid work commitment that I cannot even remember. I do remember Vin came home late that day and was obviously upset and worrying but not about himself he was worrying about me.

We had an oxygen concentrator delivered which was placed in the dining room with tubing that allowed Vin to walk to all areas of the house. I often stood on the tube when I walked past him yanking his head back. Poor man. We had two large cylinders in our coat cupboard near the stairs for emergency use. In the garage we had a large liquid oxygen tank, as big as an upright fridge freezer. Each day from the liquid oxygen tank Vin filled a portable cylinder that he carried on his back while working. Yes, my husband was chronically ill and working full time using oxygen to support his breathing.

Vin working with nasal specs that supplied his oxygen

I forgot how young he was to have such awful breathing problems.

The company he worked for didn't do a risk assessment. They refused phased returns to work post any sickness. They didn't make reasonable adjustments for him to continue his work, and he ended up working in the office at one point. He hated office work; it didn't suit Vin one bit. He informed his manager he wanted to go back on the tools. The manager wanted him to see a doctor of their choice for assessment, hoping the doctor would say "he isn't fit for work". Off Vin went oxygen on his back to be assessed by a doctor to go back on the tools. The doctor looked at Vin and asked him what he wanted. Vin explained the situation and the doctor composed a letter stating he should be allowed back on the tools but not allowed to use ladders, risk assessments and phased returns to work post any sickness must take place. Vin knew what to ask the doctor to write, his manager was furious.

I contacting the managing director to report the poor treatment he was experiencing and the lack of support he was getting from the Manchester office. At that time, I had disability rights on my contact list and documented all conversations and inappropriate discussions and actions of this Company.

We sort advice from a local solicitor who was shocked at the poor duty of care provided by his employer. More shocking was how they excluded him from meetings and celebrations. Basically, any time engineers met up as a group Vin would not be informed. Our son Paul worked for the same company and we learned about the exclusions from him. Such a terrible way to treat a sick employee.

When Vin felt unwell and had to leave work early, he felt guilty and agreed to take a £10,000 pay drop so he could work the hours he could manage. I thought this was a disgrace. His manager just couldn't cope with an unwell employee and did his utmost to get rid of him. This was a worrying time losing £10,000 a year when we were just making ends meet. More stress more worries more guilt and pegs on my line.

Vin applied for a blue badge so he could continue

working, he was refused. He couldn't walk far and often had to park a distance from his place of work. Dr Hanley told him to appeal and if that wasn't successful, he would write in support of his application, a badge would allow Vin to keep moving and working. He was issued a blue badge and the company he worked for absolutely took advantage of this and gave Vin Manchester city centre as his area of work where parking fees were the highest. Disgraceful. Some areas he worked customers would come to the car and carry his tools. Some people were thoughtful.

One day he was called into the Manchester office for a disciplinary with a director, a representative from human resources and the branch manager. Two issues were to be raised relating to his hours of work and his health. Why the company called this a disciplinary I have no idea. Vin could take a witness and a colleague Ralph accompanied him. The first issue related to Vin finishing work at 3pm rather than 5pm. Vin responded with "that is correct I finished that day at 3pm, that is what is on my time sheet and that is what we agreed I'm paid for the hours I work". They looked at each other and said "lets ignore this and move on to the second issue". Vin knew things were wrong but wondered what the manager had been saying to the Director to instigate a disciplinary. The second issue raised related to refusal to see a doctor and the request of medical notes. Now Vin was smiling, he had the letter with him that the company doctor had written. The person that had refused to see a doctor was Ralph the colleague there to witness the meeting. Ralph, spoke up and said "do you mean me because Vin went to see the doctor last month". How embarrassing, what a bad manager. This Company was an absolute disgrace I Initially thought working for a large company would have been better, but in the alarm industry it isn't the case.

With a reduction to Vins wage, I knew continuing with education would be the only way I would be able to increase my salary. What can I do now? I had achieved a diploma in Managing in Health and Social Care with the open university, plus plenty of certificates and qualifications. I had to really think about what was next.

On the 1st December 2004 staff in the NHS were graded under the Agenda for Change. This followed agreement with unions, employers and the government. The grading allocated posts to pay bands and was designed to evaluate the job not the person. In reality that wasn't true. It was implemented differently at other Trusts and posts were graded higher or lower than colleagues doing the same work.

This was all very stressful for staff especially those in unusual roles like the DAs. My job was to get the group through the process, with a result they were happy with.

We had a new manager around this time. We had more managers than any other group probably a new boss every year. I had to stand my ground and push back to get the team the correct grade. Everything was based around a reference book which described every skill required for a role. Within a couple of months, I could recite that book like an old song, the earworm that gets stuck inside your head. I knew the words that justified a higher pay grade and with the DAs, we went through each section matching them to the descriptions in the book and scoring their role. No matter how many times I changed specific levels, the role came out, at a band five. We followed the process and the group came out of their hearing as a band 3. I was furious, we appealed, of course. I thought the union representatives were supposed to be working to support staff going through the process, the unions were nothing short of a token in the room, nothing to say and nothing constructive to offer. Around 5% of staff appealed their initial banding.

Again, the appeals process varied from site to site and Trust to Trust. There were many appeals within the Trust and I can honestly say the DAs easily deserved a band five. Their appeal was won after a lot of hard work, but they were regraded to a band four not five. The group seemed happier, but I wasn't, no matter what I tried I couldn't fit their role to a band four, it always came out at a band five. However, I had achieved the two things I set out to do in this job role, I change their job title and increased their pay. I still consider that role to be a band five.

My role was changing and I was picking different

pieces of work up which meant less time with my respiratory teams. I needed more and more work. The DAs were fine, they were managing themselves. I just needed to do the pay, and their reviews plus any extra training which was very infrequent now.

I was still working with the teams and spending time at other hospitals, plus one to one training for some nurses having difficulty with venepuncture and cannulation, I was always busy.

On the ward round one day I bumped into my aunty Joan (Aubrey's Wife) she was generally unwell and waiting for test results. She had been a patient for a short while. She looked good and we had a decent catch up, I hadn't seen her for a long time. I wasn't concerned until a few days later when I went to visit her again, she had been moved to the side ward, she was dying, she had cancer. Her husband and sons were by her side. The family were really happy with the care she received and wanted to speak to one of the doctors, I think for reassurance and I asked if anyone was available to meet with them.

The registrar came and was wonderful with the family. Both the nurse and family noticed that Joan was in pain on movement, she was prescribed medication, but to be honest it wasn't needed, Joan was at the very end, dying after a couple more breaths. It was calm and peaceful.

I offered to help prepare Joan for Rose cottage. It was an honour to take care of her that day. Joan and Aubrey had been a big part of my life especially when me and Vin first met.

Occasionally I would be witness to a complaint and found myself listening to families, voicing a concern, issue or just a moan. One family asked if I would spend a little time with them to discuss their complaint. I was happy to listen to their story and was shocked to discover the angry, rude person they were describing was the ward manager. He didn't like me being involved, and his verbal and physical response to my knowledge of their complaint was really exaggerated. He didn't realise I was trying to resolve the complaint and calm the family. It became quite an issue for him and I had to refer the family to the complaint's manager for the Trust. This was just a lovely family trying to get the best care for their father. I spoke to my manager, but as usual, nothing was done or mentioned? Remember me saying managers in denial, if they could avoid dealing with problems or issues they did.

"Why bother reporting things nothing will happen or change". I did try but thinking back nothing ever really happened.

Many managers feared for their jobs and careers, if you complained you could be bullied or find yourself never being promoted, all of which prevented an improvement in patient safety. Issues that weren't addressed could be personal, being bullied, swore at ignored, sweep it under the carpet, don't mention it and it didn't happen.

A simple example of this when Vin was having a bronchoscopy, I wanted to park the car as close to the department as possible. The only parking spot in the area was across the road from the department. I dropped Vin at the door and drove to the empty space, however a car cut me up and parked in the only disabled space available. I was about to drive away when I realised it was the woman who sold newspapers and sweets from a trolley that she pushed around the hospital. I drove to her car and showed the disabled badge. Her response was "I'm fucking staff you need to find another space" she was absolutely disgusting. I asked if she had a blue badge, she just shouted profanities the whole time. Eventually she drove away and I parked in the space and caught up with my husband.

I mentioned it to my manager who completely dismissed the bad behaviour of this woman, not one bit interested and she was senior in that Trust. In my opinion a pair together the manager thought it acceptable for a member of the Trust to swear and shout at people on hospital grounds. The worst thing is that the manager dismissed it, not because she had to, she chose too. When things go wrong, our complacency, our failure to act, report and learn has created the situations that has led to the numerous scandals we read and hear about today.

Around this time DAs were doing so much more than the original Job Description (JD) I was interviewing and spent quite a bit of time rewriting the JD and training programme. I interviewed with Sylvia who was really professional and provided excellent support to the process.

There were quite a few applicants including overseas doctors, I remember one of the consultants said "don't invite them to interview", my response was I can't, they don't meet the criteria, and they didn't. The NHS has a very specific criteria that has to be met if you want an interview. All applicants must meet every aspect of the person specification along with holding the correct qualifications.

A woman called Elizabeth applied and sounded ideal for the role however she didn't turn up for the interview. I wasn't going to give up that easy, I had a chat with Sylvia and we agreed to give her a call, she hadn't received the invite letter. Typical, in those days' recruitment was very slow. After a short discussion, she agreed to interview over the telephone. She scored the highest out of the applicants and was offered and accepted the job along with Heather, who would be working at Fairfield General Hospital after training.

Elizabeth better known as Libby loved the role, it was her stepping stone like many of the DAs. When Libby left the group, she went working in the IT department on systems doctors' use. The last person I interviewed is still working as a DA at Fairfield General Hospital, Suzanne a woman with so much potential and like the others loves the role.

LONDON

In March 2004, Alison one of the DAs who supported the cardiology teams was asked to the cardiac network to talk about her job. She came to see me and I was really happy to support her. After a chat we agreed I would go and talk about the new way of working and Alison would talk about her specific role within the cardiology team. I remember every detail of this journey; we prepared two presentations and joined them onto one floppy disc and off we went to the conference at ExCel London Docklands on the 24th to the 25th March. The conference was called Excellence in Cardiac Services: A journey to improvement.

We arrived at the hotel and were booked in for two nights. This is the first time I had been to London; I know how terrible; I have only been there once since. I have great memories of Alison and our journey and experience over those two days.

Anyway, day one we were presenting and went over to the exhibition centre where we registered at the speakers' box. They were very organised; a woman took our floppy disc and asked us to follow her. She took us to a room full of hard drives, well that's what I thought they were and a man took our floppy disc. We continued to follow her into a large empty room which would hold around 380 people. "This is where you will be presenting" she said. I looked at Alison and smiled, she didn't smile back. In the corner of the room sat a man who informed us he would change our slides; we didn't have to do anything it would be all done for us.

Our instructions were, go and have a coffee and relax, but you must come back to this room as soon as the Keynote address is completed. Off we went for coffee. We were both nervous but coping in the large room which held 3,000 delegates, it was full.

Before we arrived at the exhibition, I remember telling lots of senior staff that Alison and I would be presenting this new way of working in London and do you know not one person in the Trust asked us what we were going to say. We could have said anything, this was a national conference. Thankfully the CCU sister listened to our presentation, and gave us the reassurance we needed.

We were having coffee in the huge room when the Cardiology Directorate Manager found us. "What are you two doing here" she asked. Typical NHS manager, not knowing what the left hand is doing, because they are too busy in their own world. Her face was a picture when we told her we were presenting.

The conference attendees were called into the main exhibition area and for thirty minutes Rt Hon John Reid MP, Secretary of State for Health did his keynote address. The time went very fast and the closer we got to presenting the more nervous I became. We made our way to the plenary session in the city room, where we were presenting and sat at the front. I remember the man at the back, telling us not to worry, everything would be fine, he had no idea how nervous we were.

First up was Dr Eleanor Levin presenting the Kaiser Permanante model of health care. This is an American integrated managed, care consortium, made up of interdependent health plans and hospitals. I have never forgotten the name Kaiser Permanante rather like the name Kaiser Sozey who worked for Kobayashi from the film the usual suspects. As Dr Levin finished her presentation, I looked at Alison probably for reassurance, I walked over to the lectern and began with how can I follow that, what a wonderful presentation. I then worked my way through the slides no nerves, no fear of the slides not being available, and finally it was over. Alison was up. I left the lectern asking that questions be left until the end of her presentation and I would answer anything that came up.

Alison presented really well; she was nervous but did a fantastic job.

I stood to take the questions that came thick and fast, "that's a Drs Job or a nurse Job" "does the role require registration"? I answered the question well because they had all been asked before and I sat down next to Alison sort of exhausted, she asked, "who are you and where have you put Moira and her nerves". I have no idea where my calm exterior came from that day, but for that moment in time, I was calm.

We dutifully sat through two other speakers before we left the conference and went for a well-deserved drink. Day two arrived and a tour bus round London was needed, especially for me, I hadn't seen any of it. We were a little hung over to say the least but managed to see most of the sites jumping on and off busses. With a rush at the end of the day we collected our bags from the hotel and jumped into a taxi to the railway station, we were on our way home.

There are not many people in the NHS that can say they presented at a national conference with 3,000 delegates to an audience of over 300 especially a band four and band five. We were invited back a few times but never took up the opportunity.

CONFIDENCE

As I mentioned earlier the role of the DA was changing. We were always taught to write in the patients notes leaving no spaces to prevent changes at a later point. One doctor in particular would write about five words on an A4 piece of paper, you cannot make this up, it's a legal document, that was never addressed, everyone read this on a daily basis, it was accepted as normal.

I was asked to get the DAs up to speed ready for them to transcribe take home drugs (TTOs) and re write prescriptions. One task that would really help the juniors.

The session went well with the help of an SHO. When we had finished the group went out onto the corridor where there was a buffet waiting for another training group. The DAs thought it was for them and tucked in. Not sure if I have mixed two different training sessions here. But definitely remember the buffet that wasn't ours. After speaking to the manager of pharmacy, a start date for transcribing was arranged.

A few months later, I heard on the grapevine there

was a problem. The head pharmacist complained to a consultant and this got back to me. I arranged to meet and discuss the problem. I was shocked that she hadn't addressed the issue with me before discussing it with colleagues and the shop floor.

One of the DAs had made a mistake and was upset that everyone knew about the error because pharmacy staff were all discussing it. As a curtesy the pharmacist should have come to see me first. I asked that all scripts be audited to ensure the service the DAs provided was at least as error free as the doctors. To this end the DAs put their initials in the corner of every drug prescription and TTO they transcribed. When the audit was complete it was very clear the DAs had less errors on the scripts, more accurate than the doctors, double checking everything that was written. I didn't hear any other complaints.

Quite regularly on the consultants' ward round I would be asked to fill in incident forms. The form was huge with three copies, one stayed in the book, one was sent to the department manager and the other to the governance department.

One day while completing an incident form I noticed other forms had been completed, but all copies had stayed in the book. Some incidents needed addressing, and because they hadn't been sent to the appropriate person no action had been taken. I completed another incident form and sent all copies on, there must have been ten incidents from that ward not being addressed. I can honestly say I never received feedback from an incident I completed.

One afternoon I was bleeped to the high dependency unit (HDU) and asked to cannulate a patient with hematemesis – vomiting blood. This was a rare request from HDU, the nurses there were excellent at siting cannulas. I remember asking Dr Weir "what size do you need", "two large ones the patient may be going to theatre". I inserted two of the largest cannulas the white ones, one in each arm. I remember him saying "you should have been trained to do central lines". I quite liked being the expert at something, for once.

On the ward round with a registrar one afternoon all the bleeps went off and the number was 3333. "What does that mean" the doctors were asking I said "baby abduction, we must check all areas near to us and stop anyone with a new baby". The doctor with me was amazing, we went everywhere within our area, even getting doors unlocked so we could check inside each room. The baby was found with its father, in one of the day rooms. Nice one doctor very thorough.

My favourite social secretary for the mess and one of my favourite registrars was Georges Ng Man Kwong he was the most proactive and organised many nights out, hospital balls and restaurant visits. I think I had a little crush on him. I liked him for another

193

reason, he never lost interest, he was always interested in what his patients had to say. Same for me he didn't lose concentration even when I was talking a load of rubbish. Polite, thoughtful, good fun with a quirky manner. Georges was supportive of the role and for that I'm very grateful.

One Christmas Eve I was working with a HO covering the ward round. The SHO wasn't working, I promised I would to stay with her until she was happy to go home, If I provided enough support, she may feel confident enough to leave the hospital once the patients were seen. There was an on-call team that provided senior cover but she wasn't leaving until everything was tip top, I liked that team spirit.

We were on one of the wards when the meal trolley arrived, it was pushed into the middle of the ward. We were at the top of the ward seeing patients. I noticed an elderly lady sat up in bed, dead. I tapped the doctors' arm and walk quickly to the patient. I pulled the curtains around while the doctor checked her pulse, I grabbed the lady's notes. She had died and the patients and nursing staff hadn't noticed. She wasn't for resuscitation and I thought how nice she must have drifted off watching the activity on the ward. Not a bad way to go.

One shift I recall being bleeped to a medical ward, with a plea to take blood from a patient in their care occupying the side room. As usual, I asked, "has anyone tried". The usual response would be "yes but we cannot find a vein". This time was different the nurse was asking because she was scared to take blood from this patient. On the ward I located the patient in the side room with two prison guards. The nurse told me he was scary and a rapist. That information, I didn't need to know but she offered it and now my mind was running in overdrive, "what does a rapist look like? "All that sort of crap. He was chained to the bed by his ankles and wrists.

Wouldn't it be good if you could identify rapists by their look, think of all the people who could be saved from that torture?

I collected the request card; three bottles of blood were required. I gathered the equipment, and walked into the small side room. His bed was pushed against the wall. A guard sat at the head of the bed. There wasn't any room for the other guard he sat on a chair at the end of the bed filling the wall space. I had to squeeze between the occupants of the room to take the blood. The guards were not for moving.

If ever there was a description of a rapist, that was him, lay chained in that bed. A tall man taking up the length of the bed. He had dark long hair and a beard. I told him and the guards I needed to take blood. The patient didn't move, not even his dark eyes that penetrated the wall in front of him. The guards watched me like a hawk would its prey. I would say he was the creepiest male I ever met, I cannot say whether this was because I knew what he had done or it was his appearance. I lifted his arm and put the tourniquet on. He was wiry and muscular, an athletic strong physique. My thoughts were God help the person he raped, chilling. His skin and muscles were tight, he didn't flinch when I inserted the needle, his eyes still focused on the wall. Being in that room made me feel uncomfortable and anxious but I knew someone had to take the blood and that was my job.

Occasionally you would overhear nursing staff moaning about their manager, often not very pleasant. Usually, a response to being managed or monitored. A couple of ward clerks unconstrained vitriol was often heard and I remember one of them making a complaint about a junior doctor. The ward clerk said a doctor swore at a patient. I'm sure it wasn't true. The doctor wrote a statement and discussed the complaint with her consultant. That ward clerk thrived creating issues and problems at every opportunity. I remember having to deal with the aftermath of her venom on more than one occasion. One of her preferred tricks was to show favouritism to one team and completely exclude another team. Sounds silly, but to a junior doctor that is tired, stressed and looking for support from anyone, it can be an issue. The ward clerk would often make tea and toast for one junior but she wouldn't offer it to others. She loved this sort of thing. Making sure the PC was available for her favourite team and informing others "the PC was in use forcing them to work from another area. Her manager, and she had a few couldn't manage her, she was shipped from ward to ward, managers in denial again.

When helping at a cardiac arrest, I was often the person kneeling at the side of the patient trying to site a cannula in the patient's arm, for medication and fluids. On one occasion I remember the matron standing behind me putting the fluid bag onto the drip stand. She opened the line of fluid before I had completed siting the cannula. I was still on my knees when I realised, they were wet. On checking the floor, the end of the giving set lay there fully open. The pool of saline covered my knees and the wheels on the bed. The doctor said "all clear", as he was about to shock the patient, I jumped out of the way. The matron was laughing.

Sometimes I found it difficult to hold the tears back, listening to and seeing the sad predicament patients found themselves in. Some patients never wanted to go home. I understand patients can feel safe in a hospital and the elderly have company on the wards. How sad that patients want to stay in an environment with very little to make their stay comfortable. All patients sleep on plastic covered mattresses and pillows with very thin bedding either quilts or sheets and blankets. They don't have free entertainment and often there are no headphones for the radio. The wards were built to be useful rather than attractive and comfortable with hard surfaces everywhere. The ward environment often isn't a welcoming place, it didn't make a patient feel important, but they were.

One morning while having coffee with one of the juniors in the doctor's mess, Kathy a Senior House Officer entered the room shouting and balling at a junior. I was quite shocked at her outburst, and remember telling her to calm down. She was shouting about a forty-year-old male patient who presented with haematemesis, (vomiting blood) and needed an endoscope urgently but passed away. Her outburst included not having blood results available and being unable to get hold of an on- call person. I cannot remember what she was blaming the HO for.

That evening my husband told me his cousin had died, I was shocked he was only forty. The next day I was telling Sue my colleague the sad news when she said, "do you mean DH, the patient Kathy was going mad about". this was the second time a family member had been discussed and the information was distressing.

Later that day I had to go to the morgue with one of the juniors to identify a patient going for cremation and DH was on the next tray. Sad.

I didn't pay too many visits to the morgue, but can tell you they are clean and have a certain smell, but I don't think it decomposing bodies, I think that's too early for a hospital morgue. To get into the area where the bodies are kept you went down one level in a lift. One way in and one way out. There you would be met by a bank of numbered fridge doors; a white board held the names of patients identifying which tray a patient was on. To access a patient, you would open the correct numbered door and the patient would be lay on a long flat tray. You could see all patients in the fridge, there were no tops or sides to the trays. If you needed access to a patient on the high trays you would use a lift trolley to slide the patient on, then lower them down to your level for access.

I remember one visit early in my DA role when a new junior needed to check a patient in the mortuary. She asked me for to accompany her, we were both a little nervous. On arrival in the morgue, we were alone and found our patient in one of the higher trays. The doctor wasn't using the lift trolley, she opened the door and pulled the tray straight out. She was too rushed and scared herself a little. If you pull the trays out too far, they tip and this one did and she caught her thumb. The bodies were feet first in the fridges, heads closest to the doors, when doctors checked the patients, they partially unwrapped the head and chest, to feel for a pacemaker and identify the body. Pacemakers have to be removed from patients that get cremated as they can explode.

WEDDINGS AND NIGHTS OUT

I attended quite a few weddings while working with the doctors and by far the most extravagant was Parkash Ramchandani's'. He was training to be a max fax surgeon and I loved working with him. His wedding was held in the Piccadilly hotel in Manchester City centre and our invite was to arrive at 12 noon. I was unsuitably dressed in a suit; I should have worn a sari. We arrived and entered the venue from the lift to be met by an arch of flowers with petals all over the floor. There were ice sculptures and a huge seating plan for hundreds of people. The colours and flowers were incredible. After a while Parkash arrived and called me to the side he talked me through his outfit, head dress and henna on his hands and feet, he looked fabulous in winter white and gold. We were called through to the ceremony and sat in rows as you would at any wedding, this one had garlands everywhere and absolutely massive leaves and petals on the floor. There was a band playing in the corner. The centre stage held a gazebo covered in more flowers with a fire pit in the centre, where the ritual of the wedding took place. This wasn't a short process there was an English-speaking interpreter repeating everything that was said. Drinks were offered while we watched the ceremony and people talked and made comments which I found unusual, but loved.

When the bride entered the room, she didn't walk she was carried by her brothers, they were at her side and carried her by her elbows, she was floating. It was amazing, she wore red and was covered in gold bangles and necklaces. I couldn't take my eyes off her. After the ceremony, we sat chatting to their friends and family while enjoying delicious food.

The bride and groom were not around during this time and on their return, they were wearing different outfits. The bride wore a very heavy gold brocade gown, and looked amazing. The evening guests started to arrive and I can still remember the opening of the dining room set out ready for the evening meal. The walls were black with little lights reflecting back from the glassware on the tables. The top table was long and covered almost the width of the room, it was higher than the other tables enabling the bride and groom to see all their guests. The top table was covered in large leaves and flowers forming a waterfall of colour cascading over the edge. Each table had a beautiful display and the wedding cake was made in the image of Ganesh the Deity of good fortune.

We sat in wonderful surroundings enjoying delightful

202

company, nice food and good wine. What a day, we left at midnight while the desserts were still waiting to be served as the next day Adam our nephew was being christened and we needed to get some sleep. I remember saying to Vin "it's downhill from now, no other wedding will be as good or elaborate" and I have been right so far.

The last doctors wedding I attended was between Aurelia Elliott and one of the elderly care physicians Peter McCann. Aurelia was struggling to choose music for her entrance, it had to be a song by Queen. I'm not the best at names and titles of songs but my daughter Helen has an excellent memory for these things and straight away she suggested, "find me someone to love".

Peter and Aurelia were very thoughtful, when the wedding invite arrived, they asked if were staying at the wedding venue overnight so they could allocate a room for us as there were only four bedrooms available. They were so considerate thinking of Vins health. Other memories on the day include, visiting Aurelias room before the wedding to witness a scene from the film, my big fat Greek wedding. In the film the bridesmaids are running around in spanks of all shapes and sizes. In Aurelias room one lady (not Aurellia) was wearing long- legged full-bodied hold me in gear, she was running around, in a bit of a panic about something. I can only recall the underwear; I couldn't take my eyes off it.

We sat waiting for the bride in a large conservatory built on the side of the building, I remember saying to Dr Hanley as queen started to play, she will arrive now this is her song. She looked beautiful in an off the shoulder gold dress with small red rosebuds and coming from a hairdressing family (mum and sister) I noticed her matching hair with gold highlights. Peter wore a white jacket with red tie and red and gold waistcoat. Nice wedding.

I have been lucky working with wonderful young people and enjoyed many nights out, in their company. A couple of these evenings stand out. We were booked in the Living Room bar and restaurant in Manchester for a meal. I sat next to one of the young HOs chatting waiting for others to arrive. He mentioned famous people often frequented the restaurant, especially footballers. I laughed and said "I wouldn't notice, I didn't follow football". However, my husband is a Manchester United fan and you kind of absorb football information without trying. I noticed, stood right in front of me on the other side of our table, in touching distance, David Beckham. I looked around the room and could see other United players. I couldn't name them. I turned to the Junior doctor and said "the Manchester United players are here", you should have seen his face, utter delight, and the speed he began to text everyone. As I looked round the room, I noticed TV stars as well as footballers. I was more of a fan of the Junior doctors than of lads that kicked a football round for a living. The juniors were all on their phones, it was quite a surreal image, I admired and revered the job the young junior doctors did and they looked like they valued more the boys that kicked a ball around a field. Life.

Now a weird one for you. The respiratory team were invited for dinner by one of the Junior doctors, a really pretty young woman living in a flat in the centre of Manchester. The invite for curry provided by her mum and drinks before hitting the bars in town.

On arrival I was offered a gin and tonic and sat chatting to our team Registrar. There was quiet a babble going on in the room avoiding the host. I asked "what's going on".

"Look at the pictures on the wall". It took me a while to work out what they were all looking at. In front of me along one wall was many A4 images different colours and shapes, all vaginas. What on earth was she doing. The images were not a permanent fixture because they weren't framed, they were laminated. I didn't get it. I was trying to work out if they were prints or photographs. Who had modelled for them, had she? I don't remember if anyone in the room had the confidence to ask her why she had put up the pictures and what response was she expecting. She was great though, another of my favourites we went to the registrars wedding together.

SAYING GOODBYE

In the spring of 2005, our eldest daughter Jenny announced she was moving to America with our two beautiful grandchildren Harry age three and Olivia aged one. She needed to learn to drive before she left England and had to marry Alan her long-term partner to get the required visa.

She arrived at our house one Sunday telling us she was getting married the following Saturday. We had five days to prepare. We arranged for flowers; at Debenhams she chose a gold dress. We booked a section of the restaurant in Worsley Old Hall with the local cricket club for the evening reception. I prepared table decorations and balloons. My outfit purchased the night before the wedding was too small. On the day she looked beautiful and her dad although very unwell managed to walk her into the room, his oxygen was waiting by his chair.

The wedding was successful but the whole time all I could think about was losing them to America. Her husband travelled there and rented an apartment leaving Jenny to rent there newly purchased house and pack. They stayed with us for a couple of days before leaving for the States. We were so sad one of us couldn't travel with her, to help with the babies and to settle them into the new country. Vin was needing help with a shower and dressing and I couldn't leave him. Terrible time.

These were hard times for us we missed our daughter and our grandchildren so much and it didn't help with the worry of Vins health. I remember the stress of these days so well, there was no let-up, stress watching my husband go to work and the way his employer treated him, my daughter moving away, our mum's poor health, money worries, wow I have no idea how I got up some days.

My qualifications were growing and I was recognising the new language at meetings and conferences I attended. I had my second management qualification and one in project management. I was asked to go to Fairfield General Hospital, this time not to write a report from shadowing teams but to set up a discharge lounge on one of the wards. This didn't take too long and was up and running within the week. All the times I spent at Fairfield hospital I was coming into contact with Julie Owen a Divisional Nurse Manager. I found her quite funny, she had a good sense of humour and could hold her own with even the most senior of staff. Julie was the person that saved me later on. As I said earlier, I had some lovely nights out with the teams, here are a few photos.

Cardiorespiratory girls with Sue and Jackie

Catherine one of my favourite SHOs
a gentle soul, one of the nice people
you meet in life.

SHOs – I cannot believe how young they look

Anti (SHO Antoinette Hadida) and me. Mostly I
remember her thoughtfulness.

Just how I remember Catherine and Anti
Young doctors with so much responsibility

Cheers Dr Hanley

Sylvia, Ali, Joannes daughter and me

Libby and Heather - Me, Jackie and Pat

The canal boat in Manchester for our summer night
out - CCU nurse and Jon one of the Consultants

TRAUMA STRESS AND TRANSPLANTS

I deliberately refuse to accept the truth about something unpleasant, that I know deep down in my heart, will affect me and my family. This is the description of the ostrich I had become with my head buried in the sand. I'm still a bit like that.

In the February of 2005 Vin was assessed for a lung transplant. The assessment took a week. A multitude of tests including angiogram and echocardiogram were carried out, even his teeth were checked, that was the best check-up ever. He was called back to clinic as adults with end-stage lung disease are candidates for transplant and Vin met those criteria. Basically a 50% chance of dying from his condition within two years if a transplant wasn't done.

In the March Vin received an appointment and met Professor Nizar Yonan a Cardiothoracic surgeon and clinical lead who described to Vin the risks and outcomes for different types of transplants. The best outcomes by far were liver and kidney transplants, lungs came out worse. Fifty percent of patients don't survive five years, he was told. Vin asked for a liver, the consultant didn't get his humour. He was put on the list for a double lung transplant and was given a bleep to take home. The conversations weren't that difficult when we mentioned it to family, everyone could see his struggle.

Vin used nasal specs for his oxygen, which on a good day you wouldn't notice straight away. He carried his liquid oxygen on his back while working and moving around. At home he used the concentrator, which works by drawing air into the machine and separating out the oxygen from the other gases using a filter system.

One of my scariest moments happened when I found Vin distressed trying to breathe. He couldn't get any oxygen into his system. He had overdone some activity. When I say overdone, it could have been, he tried to tie his own shoes. He couldn't breathe, at first, I thought the concentrator was broken and remember turning up the oxygen level, he was really struggling. I went to get the emergency cylinder from the coat cupboard but that wasn't the problem. When Vin struggled, no matter what amount of oxygen you gave him, nothing would happen, because no oxygen was going in. He needed to relax and rest, try watching your partner not being able to breath, it's awful and very scary. A small amount of oxygen got through, eventually he recovered and we talked about what I could have done to help. There is nothing you can do Moira I need to recover then I can breathe. He was exhausted all the time, doing the smallest of things. God, how did he manage to work, but he wouldn't stop.

We had some funny moments around this time where members of the public liked to offer Vin their opinion. He was called lazy on more than one occasion for using a lift to the first floor. One woman even said he should be ashamed of himself; a young man like him being so out of breath. He had many comments when out and about in a sign written car, parked in disabled spaces. People would knock on the window of his car including traffic wardens and tell him the space was for disabled people only. They would continue to moan "move your car someone might need the space", that space isn't for you". Even though he was wearing nasal specs and you could see a drift of vapour coming from the oxygen tank, they would continue. I could write of many occasions where inappropriate things were said to Vin and of my occasional angry responses. Vin couldn't answer, he couldn't breathe most of the time, not enough to speak anyway.

Vin was given a folder at the clinic containing information for possible transplant recipients. What he should do to prepare, make a will and stay as healthy as possible. He had to read about the notable side effects of anti-rejection drugs including: weight gain, stomach problems, facial hair, diabetes, kidney damage, osteoporosis, cancer and high blood pressure. He has all of them now and others.

217

When Vin was admitted for his initial assessment, he met the team who would be involved in his care. What an amazing group of people. Prof Yonan the surgeon, Dr Leonard his physician, Anaesthetists, Intensive care and lung specialists, transplant nurses and doctors, coordinators, Physiotherapists, Psychologists and Social Workers all played a massive part to prepare him for potential transplant.

A week after being put on the waiting list the phone rang and a none urgent voice informed us there was an available lung and Vin should make his way to the transplant centre. After a shower and unsuccessfully trying to contact the children, we got in the car. Vin drove, just the two of us then.

We were quiet, occasionally glancing at each other. I was getting upset. Work mode was the best place for my mental health, something I learned to do to protect myself. I didn't want to burst, but felt like exploding with absolute uselessness in this traumatic situation. I couldn't do anything to prevent what may occur, even though I wanted it too. I was scared.

Vin was Mr. Calm. I needed to get my emotions in check. We knew Vin would be quickly assessed and the donor lungs would be examined for suitability.

We arrived at the Jim Quick transplant ward where a bank nurse began to admit him. While putting on his name bracelet, she said "you are here for a possible double lung transplant" and looked at Vin for confirmation. He stared at me and I stared back. Reality check. The nurse had to complete a standard set of tests. Nose and throat swabs were taken, blimey she was rough. After two attempts getting his blood pressure, she struggled to find a vein to take his blood. He needed to be weighed but she couldn't use or read the scale, I had to do it. I wasn't happy. My hackles were up, I'm sure if you looked hard enough you would have seen me covered in spikes and quills. I felt like Vin wanted me to take him home but neither of us said anything. After a couple of hours, a nurse came behind the curtains and informed us the lungs were not viable and the transplant wouldn't be going ahead today. We could go home. I almost dragged him out of the hospital, such a relief.

That was the best thing that could have happened. The events of that night forced Vin to really consider what he wanted and I could see he was unsure. The next day I gave his favourite transplant co-ordinator a call, and asked her to contact Vin for a chat. I told her what had happened the previous night. He wanted to be removed from the transplant list until we had celebrated our wedding anniversary. I knew he still needed thinking time.

219

Our anniversary came and went. Vin attended clinic where the consultant showed concern for his deterioration. There was a possibility he could tip over to an unrecoverable state and transplant wouldn't work. Vin went back on the list; the bleep was back in his pocket.

We were used to bleeps, I had one for work but that didn't go off at night like Vins. His work bleep was always busy with engineers ringing for help or talking through a problem. I remember drifting in and out of sleep many nights listening to Vin trying to calm a customer down or talking shop to the engineers. I could occasionally hear customers crying, they were scared, groups of youths were hanging around their premises and they felt unsafe. I would go mad, what did they expect Vin to do, tie the oxygen tubing round their necks. He would be really calm and tell them to call the police.

When the engineers went to a really bad area, they would go in twos because if they went alone, they couldn't guarantee having a vehicle or tools on their return, the extra man was to watch the cars.

The bleep didn't go off when he had his first call for transplant, the telephone rang. Our land line became a source of stress. Our number was similar to a local taxi company and sporadically we would receive calls requesting a cab. My "wrong number" response often didn't end the call so I had to put the phone down.

On the morning of Sunday 20th November 2005, Helen our youngest daughter was at the house. I was making breakfast; we always had a cooked breakfast on a Sunday. Vin was in bed, I asked Helen to hurry her dad along. She went upstairs and ran down looking shocked, "what's happened" "it's dad, you better go and check him". I was dreading looking round the bedroom door, I thought he may have died while I was down stairs.

He looked as he always did, a pale grey with a bluish tinge around the edges. If you look at a person every day you don't tend to notice deterioration. However, if you look at photographs, you can see it, they look so unwell, and you wonder why you didn't recognise the deterioration.

Vin said he was fine, that was always his answer to "are you OK" and it still is. I went back down stairs to tell Helen all was well.

Vin arrived down stairs gasping for breath as usual. Over the years we had learned not to ask him anything until he was rested from the strain of the stairs. Slowly, he was back to normal and wearing the cardigan he kept in remembrance of his dad. That cardigan had been on the floor of the wardrobe right at the back since his father passed away, which was years ago.

I looked at him and smiled, I have no idea how he managed to get on the floor and root through the contents of that wardrobe. The day went by as normal for me and at 7:30 that evening the phone rang, one of the transplant co-ordinators asked,

"Vin, would you go as backup for a person in Ireland".

All organs had two possible recipients. Vin was happy to be back up for another patient. She said "get ready but to stay at home", she would ring back later. I gave Vin a shower and packed his bag. We waited. My feelings were shock, disbelief all wrapped up in a sense of dread. Vin was calm and had a peaceful state of readiness about him. He talked about the sadness for the family who had lost a loved one that day and the patient in Ireland who would stay on the list.

We knew the organs may not be suitable, even if he was used as backup. The transplant team had to determine the organs suitability. We could be coming home again. We didn't know what was happening at the hospital until 11pm when the co-ordinator called. Vin would definitely be the recipient of the lungs, due to fog. The flight from Ireland bringing the patient had been cancelled. The organ was being driven from Leeds to Manchester down the motorway, for my husband.

We contacted our children easily this time, but we didn't call Jenny in America until we had some news, there was nothing she could do.

Our son Paul, daughter Helen and her partner Duane were travelling to the hospital. Vin drove, my thoughts drifted to the activity in the hospital, how do they manage and coordinate the donor and the recipient, anything to get my mind off what was going to happen. I was back in work mode.

The transplant coordinators are responsible for identifying potential organs and coordinating with the national network to allocate those organs. When a deceased donor organ becomes available, they enter information onto the database. Including organ size and condition, blood and tissue type. The computer generates the match and a list of patients is produced. It is common for patients to be called about an organ offer, but placed as backup. Just in case the initial recipient wasn't available, or, as in Vins case, due to fog.

We arrived at Wythenshawe hospital at 11:30. Vin went through the usual preparation and tests for patients having major surgery. The look on his face was different from the previous call, he was more comfortable, more relaxed. We were told the anaesthetist would be with us shortly to consent Vin for his lung transplant and within minutes he was there.

That was the best consent I had ever witnessed, a list of possible things that could go wrong and the list was massive. This was a no holds barred consent, absolutely no limits to what he said. Vin looked at me and I shrugged, what could I say the risks were so high. At 11.50pm he was placed in a gown and porters and a nurse came to take him to theatre.

I followed by his side praying all would go well. We arrived at the anaesthetic room, I remember two people a consultant and his registrar YL one of the juniors from my mother ship, Wythenshawe was part of his rotation. "What are you doing here Moira", "your patient is my husband". He smiled and inserted Vins cannula then said "Moira it's time you went" I gave Vin a kiss and walked back to my children, walking away was difficult, I was so scared that would be our last farewell, I had to pause, I didn't want to fall to the floor.

I sat with my children in the outpatient's clinic listening to time tick away, I perceived it as much slower than normal, I felt cold and uncomfortable. There were bedrooms in the clinic for these moments however they were being used, but not by families. The night passed and the clinic staff were arriving. "Who's having the transplant" they asked. Everyone knew Vin at the clinic it was a nice family atmosphere. One of the nurses said she would go and check how he was. I cannot remember if she returned or if anything was said.

The coordinator let me know that the surgeon was unable to do a double lung transplant but managed a single lung. Vin would later be transferred to the transplant ICU an annex off the main ICU.

It is the weirdest thing waiting for over eight hours in an outpatient area, with the chill of the night looming heavy over the world and having the weirdest of thoughts.

Later that morning we were escorted to the ICU which we accessed via a back corridor. I realised visitors walked through the main ICU to access the transplant ICU. It had three individual rooms for Transplant patients, one nurse in each room and one on the corridor. Amazing.

I walked into the room, Vin looked dead and bloated I was shocked to see the ventilator moving pushing air into my dead husband. Helen stood on one side of the bed; I was on the other. She said "dad doesn't look good" I said he looks better from this side, we changed sides. He didn't look any different but I needed to reassure her. Paul our son, walked into the room looked at his dad turned round and took a seat on the corridor outside the room, Duane joined him. I have no idea how long we all stayed in that moment. I took a walk around the grounds and began to make phone calls.

I spent the morning so lost, drowning in such sadness, somewhere between dark and dawn. I couldn't call his mum she needed a face-to-face conversation. I called my sisters and our friends James and Karen and Vins brother. I don't recall calling anyone else.

This is where shock was setting in because I don't remember travelling home. I visited Vins mum and told her. I remember having a shower and going straight back to the hospital. They were going to ring me to come back, Vin had taken a turn for the worse but Mr. Yonan told the nurses to leave me for a while, he was still there though – he hadn't gone home. Visiting was for me and the children at first and I remember my daughter in law not being allowed to visit due to the gases which can be dangerous if you are pregnant, she was expecting our third grandchild. My youngest sister was upset because she couldn't visit. Honestly, she would have been too upset and I didn't think I would stop if she started crying.

Apparently, I travelled to our friends, Karen and James a couple of times to update them and James cooked for me, I have no memory of this. I was properly out of it, in a complete haze, with no positive thoughts. I told you right at the beginning of my book I remember the sad the unusual etc. well that's how I remember Vins transplant.

All so very sad.

I contacted work to apply for compassionate leave. Lin my manager, at the time, informed me compassionate leave is for one week and to contact my GP for a sick note. The note for one month took me up to a week before Christmas, I was given a further two sick notes.

I spent most afternoons and evenings just holding his hand. The room was quiet and always staffed by a skilled nurse. Some I liked more than others. The male nurse on that area were not my favourite because they were the ones that gave Vin the bad memories of this time and he remembers. Be careful what you say to vulnerable patients, you may think they can't hear you, or they won't remember, they do.

Most of the time I tried to stay in the moment, not letting my mind wonder down the "what if" route, what if he doesn't make it, what if he doesn't come home.

One day I arrived on the ICU and Vin looked like his dad. His hair was very greasy and combed back from his forehead, just like his father did using brill cream. I asked the nurse what was on his hair and she mentioned the cream from his toiletry bag. That was his moisturiser.

He was given a tracheostomy when they wanted to reduce his ventilation. One afternoon he tried so hard to get through to me and Helen my youngest daughter, he used letter board to give us a message. Don't go, don't leave me, don't go home.

There was fear in his eyes. OMG what has been happening. Helen and I absolutely struggled that afternoon and evening. Vin was either fully ventilated or spending a couple of hours using a machine called a Draeger which forced him to work really hard to get his new lung working. Vin would spend a couple of hours awake before he was sedated again. That was a bad day.

I remember sitting on the corridor while they did a bronchoscopy. I watched through the window and was amazed to see the stitches attaching his new lung, it was so clear. Two different tissue colours sewn together. They reduced Vins sedation to perform the bronchoscopy and he will tell you a story like Rumpelstiltskin and weaving cloth around his head. He had some weird stuff going on.

He has memories of hundreds of people marching through the room at the end of his bed wearing body suits in two colours, brown and red. Hallucinations are very common when ventilated.

I received a call from Lin my manager, my Agenda for Change (AfC) grading was the following week. I asked could the date be changed due to my situation. Her response was MC (the Director of Nursing) wanted to be on the panel and that is her only available date. Like a fool I attended the hearing. I sat outside the interview room waiting to be called in. Nobody came.

Eventually the office staff informed me MC couldn't make it. Absolutely disgusting treating a member of staff this way. Thoughtless.

Eventually my post was processed through the grading system and I was matched to a band 5 biomedical scientist, ridiculous.
I didn't care at this point what they matched me to. Years later I attending a conference and MC was present. During lunch, I waited until she was seated and sat as close to her as I could. I started to chat, "do you remember me" she obviously didn't have a clue who I was but why should she. I told her and everyone around that table my story. Again, on the side of humanity, I hope she didn't realise the result of her actions, she didn't apologise or say anything. Another manager in denial and void of empathy, she just looked at me, I picked up my lunch and moved seats.

It was weeks before I slowly surfaced from the nightmare, I seemed to be living a weird existence. At first the darkness was all consuming, there was no light. Then a glimmer of hope. Although he was ventilated, occasionally I would see him chewing the tube in his mouth. His sedation must have been reduced. I knew he was there.

My favourite moment, came the day they removed his tracky. I walked into his ICU room, gave him a kiss and start chatting about nothing, while putting clean towels in his cupboard. It was difficult to talk about anything because nothing was happening. I was spending my day travelling to and from the hospital and updating anyone that rang me, that was it. After about five minutes I sat on a chair at his side. He spoke, that was the best sound I had heard in such a long time. I remember putting his birthday cards up in ICU mid-December, he wasn't interested. He was however interested in a TV programme called Egg Heads, as soon as he could speak, he asked the nurse to put the programme on. He may have been ventilated for most of the day but on the hours, he was awake working hard to inflate the new lung, he enjoyed his quiz show.

Vin was in hospital for weeks, four of those weeks on ICU. On Christmas Eve we took him home for a two- day trial. He was so weak. That was difficult, he must have been scared with just me to rely on, rather than the fantastic team at the hospital. We have managed from that day to this. He is such a strong man mentally as well as physically. I would have been dead years ago if I had suffered the way he has.

I returned to work when I felt comfortable leaving him home alone. When Vin was ready to go back to work, he rang the office in Manchester and asked for the return of his company car.

A couple of days after Vin had his transplant the company took his car away, not a thought if I needed it. They drove it away without a word. During Vins sick leave I didn't receive a call asking how he was. They didn't send a card for him. They wrote him off. An absolute disgrace. The company initially didn't want to do a phased return to work either. Vin went back to work for a short period. The transplant hadn't given him back the life he missed, it gave him a new life, different, but one we would get used too. He still doesn't admit his struggle and replies "I'm Ok".

LAUGHTER AND NEW FRIENDS

I slotted back into my routine at work but my role had changed so much over the past few years. I still supported the junior teams and took part in Trust inductions, along with other pieces of work I got roped into doing. The DAs had written survival guides for their specialty and each year along with one of the juniors these were updated. I think the last one I updated was with Ed Parkin in 2007. The guides provided useful tips for HOs to survive their first job. The information supported the juniors first week and included what everyone failed to mention at induction, like the code for the doctors' mess! The guides told the juniors about the personal foibles of their consultants. Occasionally I had to alter them, so they didn't offend.

I knew it was time to move on, but to do this I needed Masters level qualifications and Dr Hanley helped me with half the fees from a training endowment fund which I'm eternally grateful for. I enrolled with Huddersfield University, at the Business school based at Oldham on an MBA course.

I remember my nerves the day I walked into the

classroom. I met one very chirpy tutor Barbara and an amazing group of people.

My group out of the cohort were Debbie who arrived late on the first day, a tall dark-haired woman, she looked the business. Dawn the comedian of our group and like Debbie worked in the NHS, she was quite senior but not the psycho sort, thank God. I can reliably say it physically hurts to be in her company, because of the laughter. She was excellent with ideas and keeping me focused. Another person who pushed and pulled me through the course was Coral. She was my rock and if I struggled, she was happy to spend her time sorting my head out, and she did, on many occasions. I sat next to Coral, she's about the same age as my eldest daughter. A director of her own company that made mezzanine floors, an Engineer. I was impressed, she was bright, intelligent a good listener and excellent friend. My nights out with Coral still consist of good food, wine and G&Ts usually in Prestwich. Love this lady.

Diane, another of our group and senior in the police was a late finisher completing her assignments just before they were due, I was a plodder a bit here and a bit there, but we both completed. I laughed my way through two years attending classes every week and working at home every Saturday.

Finally, in 2007 I got to wear a cap and gown, even that didn't go smoothly. The company providing the graduation garb gave us gowns for a degree qualification instead of post graduate gowns. I didn't notice any difference; they were all changed. I didn't mind, I looked a mess in it anyway the colours and shape of the top wouldn't improve the way I looked.

The laughter was back in my life and I enjoyed the time with the group. I had masters level qualifications in Strategic Management and Leadership.

Me Coral, Dawn, Debbie and Dave

Those two years were good for me, a little normality after years of stress and strain. The course work was difficult while doing a full-time job plus everything else that was going on at home, it was definitely one of my best experiences though.

Working with Drs Hanley and Weirs teams were my benchmark for what efficient effective ward rounds, and patient management looked like. I was asked to shadow a couple of medical teams and spend some time on their wards to establish who completed the jobs DAs performed at the mother ship. We were looking at introducing DAs at other hospitals. Shadowing colleagues and documenting who does what can be time consuming. I had witnessed so much hospital activity that I could easily see where the consultant teams could use the help of the DAs.

At one hospital I met an amazing consultant physician, with fantastic teaching skills, on one of the post take ward rounds. You could see the juniors enjoyed the way he worked and how he explained his way of working. I enjoyed shadowing that team, I was learning too. However, the consultant completed the jobs normally undertaken by Junior doctors or DAs.

On another ward I witnessed ward rounds that did not match the benchmark I had from years of attending rounds with respiratory Consultants. Everything I collated was documented in the form of a report and given to my manager. She had to decide what to do from the options and conclusions I gave her.

This hospital site was much smaller than the mother ship, everyone seemed to know everyone by name. We did introduce DAs there working with the medical teams and they were very successful.

I was back with my teams, my mother ship, back in the office just off the doctors' mess, getting my visits from Elaine the Secretarial Manager. Elaine was the most qualified administration person I met during my career. She not only had secretarial and administration qualifications but two masters' degrees one MBA the other in Law and Ethics. She was a band 5 but her role was a band five and she needed to apply for roles with a higher banding, same as me.

Any time we met for a coffee we would have discussions about moving on, we were always talking ourselves out of our jobs every week.

The Trust were introducing digital dictation for patients' letters and secretaries and doctors needed to be using the equipment by a specific date. Elaine and I trained them on the details of the new equipment installed throughout the Trust. We held teaching sessions in groups and individually while collaborating with the IT department who installed the equipment. Most doctors and secretaries completely understood and required one session. Others needed to be reminded more than a couple of times. We visited the hospitals meeting amazing staff, I enjoyed my days working with Elaine, she is one of those nice people that you cannot find fault with.

The DAs were now proficient at rewriting prescriptions and transcribing TTOs and dictating discharge letters on the analogue system. The DAs involved themselves in every aspect of their specialty on the ward and within the departments. What a fantastic job we all had.

Again, my role began to change and I was asked to support other teams who were struggling, I found myself working half a day with an elderly consultant who had been fraught covering two wards, with no junior staff. Many an afternoon he would chase me down to complain he was being bullied and could I deal with it for him. I didn't feel he was supported by his colleagues, at consultant level. He wasn't a young man but if he was having problems the specialty Consultants should have supported him.

Eventually, I went to the Medical Director and passed the information on. I had tried to mediate but staff on the wards didn't recognise their bullying manner. He wasn't going to get anywhere. I spent half a day doing his TTOs and rewriting any scripts for two wards. I bled every patient that needed it as the phlebotomists didn't attend every day and when they did, I was back up for them too. He couldn't cannulate and I took over from him after witnessing one attempt, if I wasn't around, he called the specialist nurses and they obliged.

When I left those wards and supporting the consultant, I gave him the ophthalmoscope I had been issued. My stethoscope went to a registrar called Simon Bailey. I missed working with the respiratory teams. I felt I was on my own on these wards. I was getting bored and needed to be challenged much more. Working with a consultant with no Junior doctors removed me from a role where I got the most satisfaction. I complained to my manager and asked for help while looking for another role. She contacted Julie at FGH and off I went again.

I remember the call, asking if I would support a ward at another hospital. I would be leaving my medical teams on a more permanent basis. The manager of the ward had been put on gardening leave. I understood the request as over the years I had built a good team.

A junior sister was to stand in for the band 7 but needed further support organising the ward and improving communication. My first task was to clear all incidents that had been overlooked or not investigated. I was given access to a list of incidents and complaints and began requesting sets of notes to get me started. My role was to investigate, gather evidence and report on incidents following the various policies and procedural structures involved. The incidents required investigation as they had occurred in the care provided on that ward.

The Trust had a good reporting tool for incidents and I needed to look at the sources of data that had been recorded and occasionally interview staff, noting those involved or impacted by the event, finally documenting my findings.

For each incident, I had to look up old policies and procedures to ensure I was looking at the correct documents for the time of the incident. Things do go wrong in a care setting and it is vital these incidents are recorded to ensure learning takes place and providing assurance it won't happen again. My job was working out what went wrong and why it had gone wrong, then I informed Julie, she used the information to provide sustainable actions locally on the ward to reduce the risk of similar incidents occurring again.

At first, I was concerned my opinion might not be what Julie wanted to hear. Different reviewers have different opinions about problems in care and I wasn't sure how in- depth she wanted me to be. I understood that many managers are committed to a blame culture and that wasn't how I worked or thought. I needed to know that Julie wasn't just looking to point the finger and lay blame at someone's feet.

Mistakes are made, something can be overlooked or miscalculated, people do get tired and distracted and suddenly they find themselves being investigated with the possibility of losing their job. I always completed a thorough investigation and Julie fully supported me, I had been worrying unnecessarily.

I really got into this new aspect of my role and enjoyed reviewing and analysing the incidents hoping to improve patient safety. I was working from the sister's office which was situated outside the ward at the end of a corridor, which I thought, very strange, a sister's office should be within a ward area, not outside and off another corridor. You could see things hadn't been going well, notice boards were very out of date, many with no information on. Staff were not as informed and meetings to address issues hadn't taken place. The weeks and months went by and I was enjoying the work, it was a smaller hospital and the staff were extremely friendly.

I was up to date with the incidents and Julie thanked me for helping, that was probably the first thank you I ever got in the NHS, she asked if I would help on a ward to build a team and improve communication, but first would I join a matron with the initiative "releasing time to care: the productive ward.

This initiative like many others I witnessed and worked on were labelled as, innovative ways of working. The programme said it is a systematic approach to improving the reliability, safety and efficiency of care. Over the years I have been involved in the Productive ward, well organised ward, Listening into Action, Verendern rapid process improvement to name but a few, all to make the work efficient. Basically, reorganise your work area, reduce waste and walking, and searching for equipment. Know your patient status, how your ward is doing, all at a glance. That's the mantra.

This is where Collette Parker came in, the matron, she was worth every penny to that hospital. What a worker and what a talker, you didn't get a word in edgeways, she spoke so fact and had amazing knowledge, I liked her she was extremely patient focused and I loved that. The staff were very nervous of her you could see it when she entered the ward, but that was OK, I felt they needed a jolt into the reality of the condition their ward was in and it was no body's fault but theirs.

Collette ordered large cages for rubbish and out of date stores to be removed. I cannot tell you how many cages we needed but it took weeks and I still remember her showing me a sink that had been discovered under the stores in the clinical room and staff apparently didn't even know it was there. How bad is that.

The staff were lovely but had become complacent and that needed to change. I worked really hard on that ward introducing monthly bulletins, creating up to date information for all the notice boards. We purchased new trolleys to put equipment closer to hand for nurses. We introduced monthly meetings for staff involving them in making improvements and changes to the ward, things were working and the area had improved so much it looked and felt like a different ward.

Just before I left, Collette mentioned a position that had become available which she said would suit me down to the ground, I had already seen the advert for an Access Booking and Choice (ABC) Manager but I wasn't keen on the position, it wasn't my sort of thing. I was more than qualified to apply for the post but really unsure. It took a couple of days reading this wishy-washy job description absolutely nothing compared to the job description (JD) I currently had, this was a grade higher a Band 6. I'm going for it, what's the worst that can happen.

I rang the department and made arrangement to pay them a visit and speak to the current manager. I discovered a band eight was currently doing the job, the previous band six left months back.

The department was fine, based on one of the converted nightingale wards, a large open plan office with one individual office at the top and bottom of the old ward. The office wasn't very noisy and the staff working there were curious when I arrived. I'm sure they would have researched who I was and where I had been working. After talking to the manager, I discovered there were two management positions available one in Rochdale and one at the mother ship. I remember talking to Elaine about the posts and we both decided to apply for the positions. We were given interviews. Elaine was successful and was offered a post at Rochdale, I was offered the post at my mother ship, a band 6 position.

I have a lovely memory of me and Elaine sitting in my office in the doctors' mess laughing at the JD, it was more like a supervisor's post, than a managers' little or no responsibility was written into the plan and this was a grade higher.

The decision was made I accepted the post.

I was leaving my junior doctors and my favourite ever role, but needs must and all that. This was a very sad work time for me. New horizons were screaming out and I suppose my role had changed and I couldn't go back.

A huge thank you to all the Junior doctors for teaching me, for being caring and sympathetic to our wonderful patients and their families and for not laughing at me while I learned and followed you like a puppy. Thanks for all the wonderful nights I enjoyed your company and for the laughter, cheers.

Big thank you to Drs Hanley and Weir for allowing me to witness, participate and hopefully improve your ward rounds.

TARGETS SPREADSHEETS AND REPORTS

On the first day in my new role, I sat with my manager. My first impression, she was trying to teach me the clerks' job, but I was supposed to be the manager of the department, I was confused. I stayed that way for a long time. She used the exact same induction pack she used for new clerks; a completely different pact should have been available for us. My memory of this time was so mixed, I thought the band eight was really nice, she was smart, funny and appeared happy in her role. But what was her role this is where I found things difficult.

My first job was to get to know the team, I needed to know who they were and which consultant they scheduled for. My manager wanted me to become proficient in "doing the do" including the complexity of the PAS (patient administration) and TIMS (theatre management) systems, where all patient episodes and information are stored, to me that was the clerk's role not the managers. Hated it, but it was important to have a little knowledge.

The clerks were supervised by an extremely efficient woman Tracy, she checked waiting lists and supported the teams when required. I was provided with information on patients that had waited a long time for their operation, this information was cascaded up. Who was up, my manager a band 8a, directorate managers band 8a and 8b, waiting list co-ordinators band 6, their manager band? A director band? This is a lot of money. Why weren't the clerks' managed and sat with the directorate managers that worked with the consultants the clerks scheduled for. That would reduce the cost by removing so many levels of management and supervision. The cost savings would be massive.

The clerks really only needed pressure from one person not multiple people at multiple levels, no wonder they were very stressed. Absolutely ridiculous, I really struggled with the hierarchy in this department, too many managers by far. After a while my manager moved out of her office and joined the other well-paid staff who based themselves in offices off the canteen corridor, away from the ABC department. Still don't know what they did, but they were expensive.

I remember one afternoon being given the personnel file for one of my team. The file had probably been on a shelf in a back office for a while. The 'P' files were stored in my office and I hadn't noticed any were missing but then I hadn't been through them. I was shocked to discover what the previous department managers considered a capability issue. There were unusual incidents documented in the file and most things seemed to have been kept for an overly long periods of time.

Capability policies and procedures are designed to deal with those employees really lacking in an area of knowledge or ability to carry out their role. This poor woman had made a simple error, pressing the wrong button on a computer which sent the wrong clinic letter to a couple of patients. I got the shredder out and went through all staff files removing out of date disciplinaries and capability information. WOW talk about blame culture. There were many documents to shred in most files.

My manager started to put this sort of crap in my 'P' file too, I had access to it, I had been in post for two weeks. The blame culture was rife and I knew somewhere along the line bullying would be witnessed. The seniors in that department had favourites and family friends were given promotions and one to one training, the only saving grace for me was the clerks. Obviously, I was the wrong woman for the job, don't get me wrong I liked my line manager she was a nice woman and really funny but she had pressure from her manager. She was a great story teller though and I had many laughs in her company.

Part of my team were clerks that worked in the reception for the pre op clinic near to the theatres. How that came about I have no idea; they should have been part of the pre op team and managed by them. Many management issues that should have been changed years ago.

I had a choice of offices when my manager moved out, I stayed in the office at the bottom of the department, the old sluice from when it was a ward. The main office was kitted out really well, carpeted with banks of desks in groups of four down the left-hand side and single desks along the wall to the right. If I left my door open which I frequently did, I could hear most things from the office, the sound travelled right to the bottom of that department. I had lots of laughs listening to the clerks.

I was shocked at the amount of knowledge this team had and pleased to see how caring they were for the patients they helped. Yes, administration staff showing real concern for patients they never meet. How nice is that. Many a time clerks would be in early or staying late to ensure a patient was provided with the correct information or booked on to an appropriate slot.

One afternoon whilst looking at the clerks from the office I could see four consultants sat with them scheduling more patients to their theatre lists. They sat on the floor and on chairs and one on a stool. I could see they had excellent working relationships; they were accurate and knowledgeable and had this sort of methodical way of working. I admired the way they worked; they had an excellent confident telephone manner. I could listen to the hubbub of that office for ages.

When a mistake had been made and a patient arrived on the wrong date or time, the consultants would ring the clerks and insist that they speak to a manager. They were often hostile on the telephone demanding a manager to shout at. I was always happy to go and see consultants and patients when things had gone wrong. The consultants were just full of bluster but face to face they were all absolutely fine. The patients were a different matter, to them I really apologised for the wasted journey or the mis information. Now another manager would have added that to the disciplinary pile but I knew how hard and fast this team worked and I wasn't going to rage at them, I had big shoulders and that was what I got paid for.

We tried as a team to reduce any errors and they became so few the systems that were in place were working. I remember checking the work of a clerk and the letters they sent out as everything had a code so you knew if an error had been made. Unfortunately, I didn't have the speed of the clerks so doing a checking task for me was so time consuming. The supervisor did random checks so I rarely had to apologise to patients.

Each week I met with the theatre manager to check each lists capacity. Could another patient be added? It was rare a clerk would leave enough time on a theatre list to add another patient. Every operation had a time and the clerks filled lists by time. Another meeting took place each week where every theatre session was discussed, again this was to establish availability of lists.

A consultant may be on annual or sick leave freeing up a theatre, another team may be able to use it. These meeting were really funny, theatre managers, waiting list co-ordinators, me, anaesthetist and the occasional surgeon. Basically, it was like calling bingo, if a theatre wasn't being used because a consultant was away, the first waiting list co-ordinator to say "we will have that one" would get the theatre slots which helped reduce waiting lists. At this point the theatre managers would be checking if that theatre was suitable for the specialty wanting to use it. Complicated, it wasn't, I marked on my bingo card which specialty would have the slots and I passed the information to the clerks. They would add patients to the new list. Anyone of the clerks could have attended that meeting.

The major thing in this department were waiting lists, we are talking about thousands of patients. A few consultants had other lists, not on the system but within their own personal diary. Getting the consultants to give up their diaries was not that easy.

252

Then there was always a large backlog and these were often managed by waiting list initiative clinics (WLI) that ran at weekend. More money being spent, I remember hearing (possibly gossip) about a consultant that had earned £180,000 a year on top of his normal salary for doing WLI at weekend. That information came from a waiting list coordinator.

It was quite unfair because many consultants maintained a good waiting list. Others were probably working the system. I don't blame them; management allowed and authorised these lists. I witnessed that every week in that department. The clerks would tell me they have weekend lists to fill, at the very last minute, letters often needed to be delivered by taxi, Royal mail wouldn't have made it in time.

The office was long and the thermostat for the room temperature was outside my office. There were male and female clerks of different ages. I began noticing the temperature was either cool or really too warm and rang a friend in the estates department to ask "what is the most ambient temperature for an office", "21 degrees". I reset the thermostat and watched as the older women turned it down and the younger members turned it up. There were fans for those that were too warm and for the others, they had to put a jumper on. It was quite funny watching them respond to a sign I put up, telling them to leave the thermostat alone. Yes of course they altered it, and I changed it every time I walked into the room.

I was just beginning to get the hang of this weird job, when a merger was being discussed resulting in the four Access Booking and Choice departments and the Trust Contact Centre centralising to form one department at Rochdale Infirmary. The idea was to provide a single point of contact for inpatients, outpatients and diagnostics. The department was to be called booking and scheduling and would deal with all inpatient and outpatient appointments across the Trust's four hospitals at North Manchester, Fairfield General, The Royal Oldham and Rochdale.

The department consisted of 100 staff who received and dealt with approximately one thousand five hundred telephone calls per day and arranged around 960,000 appointments for patients a year. Hope I have got those numbers right. The department was located on the top floor, level D at Rochdale Infirmary. We would move into temporary accommodation on old wards with adjoining corridors. The new offices would be built once the move had taken place. I noticed my manager from the ABC department was more and more absent from everything, she was being manoeuvred out of her post. Meetings were happening on a regular basis and she wasn't there. I remember very little response when we asked where she was. I began to notice managers from other areas were more involved and took the lead on this massive transfer.

The planning for this move was excellent and every aspect of that move was well thought out and organised. I knew I would be building a team if I stayed. First of all, we needed to find out which staff were moving into the new department.

The clerks were not happy and I understood, many lived local to Crumpsall and Rochdale wasn't around the corner, it's a motorway drive and not everyone had a car. Keeping morale up was difficult at this time and I began to introduce games and activities when we had our meetings. Within groups they organised themselves offering to transport each other to and from the hospital. What team work. Others didn't want to come at all.

I remember the spreadsheets with details of staff, how many hours they worked what their specialty was, where they lived. I had to interview each individual to establish their expectations. The consultants weren't happy and I understood this too, the move would destroy their working relationships.

This reconfiguration and reallocation of work would save money. The idea that every clerk would be able to fill an outpatient clinic or theatre list on any site. They would deal with all other aspects of work within the new department. All of which could have been achieved if the clerks were moved to sit with the specialty Directorate Managers.

With my band six colleagues we began to interview

all staff, we needed around 100 members of the current teams to move with us. I was lucky, I had little experience of many clerks and can honestly say they were fair interviews. I remember one woman interviewed really well, I commented on this when she left the room, the others on the panel said "yes but her work is rubbish," what do you do?

We offered the successful clerks' jobs and the others would be reallocated to another role within the Trust, at a site of their choice.

Sitting in the empty office one afternoon I called staff in one at a time to inform them if they were moving to Rochdale or not. One clerk started to cry, she wasn't successful and as I went to comfort her, she laughed and said "thank God I don't want to go there anyway". Let me tell you we lost a good clerk she ended up becoming a secretary at Trust HQ.

There were a couple of clerks that weren't successful at interview. However, they were amazing at their jobs and the department would struggle without their knowledge and skills. We had to bring them back in and offer them a position. I would have told management to piss off, but the clerks liked their jobs and were good at it.

My manager had gone, I think she was more than encouraged to take severance. It was time to interview staff at my level. An external woman was employed to oversee the whole move. I remember asking her if she needed managers experienced in the systems, or team builders. She wanted the managers to be good at teambuilding and organising. I was OK they were my skills I was happy to put myself through the interview process.

The process for the day included presentations, interviews, a test on waiting list and teamworking through a situation. The day took an age to pass and I can recall discussing with the others being interviewed, how we felt about each station within the interview process. There were three positions up for grabs. One outpatient manager and two ABC managers were successful. I was shocked to be given one of the positions over others with much more experience but I knew they needed team builders, so for now, I would do.

We packed our ABC office up at close of play on a Friday. The very large cannon printers were to follow. Staff worked the weekend getting the department ready for work on Monday morning. I placed myself in the largest of the rooms with around ten members of my team. I had many new clerks all very experienced in their own area. We had a common purpose, be ready for the patients on Monday.

I hadn't come across some aspects of the work I was now managing, as the teams came from a variety of areas. Thank goodness I could set up a team.

My first task, was to identify what everyone could do and remember calling the ladies from the Silver Heart Unit to support and teach clerks aspects of their role. They spent days sitting with each individual spreading the knowledge. One of the clerks Dawn had work that was last to be shared and I cannot remember why. The ABC girls were straight onto teaching the others, I was really pleased they were an amazing bunch. The clerks had worked together for many years and were very relaxed with each other and easily included the new faces into their community. I still couldn't "do the do" but I had a fantastic team who could and for me that was my role, keeping the clerks happy.

It took me a while to get to know everyone, lots of tears and tantrums. It was a challenging time for them and I knew things would eventually sort themselves out, but it never did for me. There were many reporting and monitoring systems in that department, phones, lists, letters, cancellations, referrals, faxes. Not for me.

We moved into the newly designed area with long desks and partitions between each desk. We allocated the seating plans to match the work of the clerks, we didn't ask them if they had a preference, how sad the teams had very little input.

Vin wasn't in the best of health again and his prognosis post-transplant was five years. I was always worrying. One of the band six's that was successful in the reconfiguration left her role, gossip didn't get to me and I ended up being given more staff to manage and more paperwork to monitor.

Senior management reduced the band six numbers massively and were ready to promote others in the department into new band six positions. I witnessed a member of the team going from a band 2 to a band six in a few years. I'm not saying she couldn't do the job, she could, she was excellent, others were too. However, they didn't have family friends in senior positions. No comment.

My favourite memories with the clerks were at our monthly meetings. This is where I tried to improve morale with games and quizzes. At first, we weren't receptive enough to the clerks' preference for where they sat and the work they did. The work was moved from clerk to clerk after most of our manager meetings, due to staffing issues and backlogs. Good clerks should be treasured, they are very skilled workers. We should have recognised and celebrated their progress much more. I know I tried, but I felt alone the other manager was very different to me. I liked her, but her style was different. My style was sort of democratic I liked the clerks to get involved in making decisions. My colleague was a little autocratic, a persuasive style of manager, she controlled the decision making much more. She had a better awareness of the clerks' work. I suppose if I had enjoyed the role more, we could have made a good team working together.

The clerks spoke to patients every day and were often under stress with extra lists and more work. The work never went down, if they were good or speedy "give them more. The mantra in the department was always give them more". I think that is sad, they worked very hard some faster than others but that's human nature. They were micromanaged, I should have been stronger for that team they were the best.

The worst job in the department was the supervisor role, low pay, hassle from above and below. I was getting more dissatisfied with my role. I remember meeting with other managers when a colleague bragged, she never authorised compassionate or special leave for her team ever, as though it had a corresponding value attached to it. I was shocked.

A band seven joined the department and I was to report to her, another level of management? I grew tired of watching the manipulative behaviour of one of the seniors in the department. She would pick a clerk and boost them up only to drop them like a brick at her whim. The department manager Janet was Ok I liked her; in different circumstances we could have been good friends. She was calm and down to earth.

She didn't say, but I bet she worked her way through the banding over many years before she achieved her current role. She knew everyone's job and I felt a good choice for managing that department.

One of the seniors in the department was very passive aggressive, just because she could, didn't mean she should, but she always did.

I remember apologising to the new band seven for being awful when she arrived in the department. She was another I felt wholeheartedly embraced the fear-based culture, not that she was promoted for being capable of doing whatever it was she did. She was just another person to poke the clerks and I let her know what I thought. I was wrong, the clerks told me she had been Ok and wasn't the ogre they thought. I went out of my way to apologise for my thoughts and anything I said. She accepted my apology. I just didn't want to be there and often would find myself angry or in tears most days and looking for a new role at every opportunity.

It was a fear-based workplace where everyone focused on very specific daily tasks, where allocating and assigning work, measuring results, punishing tiny errors are all done to maintain order. In a fear-based culture you don't get collaboration or innovation out of people.

The clerks would inform me if they felt under pressure to change information on the waiting list and after a couple of clerks discussed similar requests with me, I reported it. Talk about setting the cat amongst the pigeons. A test was set up for all supervisors and managers. It would establish if knowledge in the department was consistent with waiting list management and Trust policy, the rules of engagement for that department. We all took the test including those that wrote the test. I had a dentist appointment and sat my test alone. I don't think the results were great but as I said earlier the clerks managed the waiting lists and the managers reacted to the information clerks gave them. The clerks would have achieved 100%, I'm sure. I cannot remember how poor my score was, it didn't concern me, I still considered my role related to keeping a large team together to meet the patients' needs. Too many of us failed that test.

It was obvious I wasn't happy, but continued to support my team. Then one day I was saved by Julie. She came to visit me in the department and I told her about my miserable job and how unhappy it was making me. Julie had a discussion with the Chief Executive requesting extra staff to support her in a new initiative called Listening into Action. Within a couple of weeks my PC and printer were packed up and moved with me to Fairfield to join her team. Eventually the funding for my post at B&S was move over too. I wished them all well.

The B&S clerks gave me a wonderful send off, and I'm grateful for all their support, such nice people. Do you remember at the beginning of the book I talked about many good-hearted staff, all with so much to give to a system that often lets them down and never getting wrong who the good people were? Well, that is what those ABC and B&S clerks were, good people and damned hard workers.

PARTY TIME AND INSPECTIONS

The Listening into Action (LiA) office situated on the ground floor of the Education Centre at Fairfield General Hospital was the base for the small team just three people Julie Owen, Lynn Rigby and now me, Vanessa joined us later. The office was calm and professional but also fun, laughter was back and lots of it. My desk and office space had been prepared, thanks Lynn.

It was lovely to feel wanted, our desire to be appreciated goes way beyond feeling nice, it's a basic need and one that is vital to our emotional wellbeing a desire at the core of who we are, to feel of value and respected meant so much to me. The role provided me with an impression that others respected me and valued my work and I was always a grafter, something I hadn't sensed from senior staff since leaving the Consultants and their junior teams.

I even had a shorter distance to drive to work against

the normal busy flow of traffic, I felt so lucky. Lynne and Julie gave me a wonderful warm welcome. Lynn a nice easy-going woman, had a delightful manner and great skills, gained from a secretarial background in the Trust. She was witty, friendly and with Julie made my move, stress free.

Julie gave me plenty of time to absorb the LiA literature gaining an understanding of my role within the team. Presenting to large audiences and supporting small teams would be the main part of the role. Everything related to staff and patient involvement, team empowerment, around challenges faced by patients and staff. Improving outcomes was the overall goal. Just my cup of tea. I could have kissed them both being back working with doctors, nurses, patients and families, the tears stopped.

Our first task was a pulse check to allow colleagues to voice issues around areas for improvement. We advertised what we were doing and had some early quick wins.

The rooms we used for the presentations ranged in size holding from twenty people to a couple of hundred. These rooms were set up almost like a social event, a party with balloons, music, tables, snacks and freebies. Our thinking was feed them and they will come and they did. Many of our large sessions were at breakfast or lunch time.

266

The sessions created a flow of ideas for improvement, there were no boundaries everything was documented. Nothing was omitted. Lynne typed the session capturing the mood of the room. We themed everything that was mentioned or documented and made a graphical representation of the information. Volunteers ran small groups making the improvements happen, they selected a topic from the ideas collected and identified staff that would support them. We arranged and booked rooms, food and equipment and prepared many presentations and posters. We advertised and wrote bulletins. A couple of questions were always asked, the main one related to what gets in the way of the chosen topic happening. I was enjoying this role it was diverse and gave me contact with so many departments within the Trust and over multiple sites.

We had some amazing and occasionally funny conversations at the sessions, one I remember related to salary sacrifice and this scheme would allow the purchase of goods before income tax was deducted from pay. Staff that attended the session discussed what they would like to be included in the scheme. It was the funniest thing reading the requests for inclusion, plastic surgery, food shopping, holidays, gas and electricity bills, basically everything from hairdressing and beauty treatments to gifts, household and white goods.

People saw a way to reduce their tax and wanted everything they buy put on the scheme. John who ran the group was successful and bikes, computers, phones and car parking all could be purchased that way.

I volunteered to run a couple of small groups myself and reduced clinic wait times for one specialty, start small then spread were my thoughts. I hope the clinic is working as efficiently today.

One large session I was running had public and staff involvement. Part of my role was to present each speaker to the audience, unfortunately, at the most crucial time I forgot the name of the person I was introducing, I'm rubbish at remembering names. I began to prattle on trying to recall such an unforgettable name, no luck.

I apologised to the audience for burbling on and introduced him by saying the next speaker will have a much better memory and pointed towards him. He stood and said "You have forgotten my name haven't you" "yes".

I remember it now Vic Crumbleholme.

For most of the small sponsor groups, the incentive for joining was not only being part of a team but learning how to present and motivate themselves and encourage others. They were all fantastic because a lot of what they did was in their own time, how altruistic.

Our small team were enjoying every aspect of this role and could really see the benefit for the Trust. We met with the CEO regularly and Julie would be pulled into other work which took her away from her lead roll. At one point she was asked to check for evidence of an infamous person having contact at one of our hospital sites. This work took both her and Lynn away from the office, leaving me with the day to day running of the groups. It was around this time I noticed we were getting a lot of staff asking to speak to us about bullying and harassment issues.

The first staff member to contact me spent a while in the office just talking about where she worked and the problems she was experiencing, I offered my opinion but realised my role was as a sounding board, that was absolutely fine, if that's what she needed. After a couple of these approaches, I decided to train as a dignity at work advisor and a Trust mediator, something I should have done much earlier in my career.

Many staff feel they are bullied and I witnessed it on more than one occasion myself, however very few would let me register the incident and no one wanted the issue taken further. I was the sounding board just like before and that was OK. No wonder bullying continues, staff are scared.

I remember mediating for a couple of departments and often the staff causing the problem didn't recognise the issue, mediation and moving on was difficult. I hope their issues resolved, because you don't get feedback you just don't know if any of your listening worked.

In 2013 the year we had the best response to a staff survey, our small team received an award for the support function of the year and a certificate of appreciation from the CEO. Our team had engaged with staff and encouraged them to complete the survey, that was all it took to get a good response, staff engagement.

It wasn't all successful, I remember sending out 100s of invitations to patients to join us for afternoon tea to discuss improvements from a patients' perspective. The room was set up, tea and cakes ready. The presentation turned on, we waited. Eventually four people arrived. We were so disappointed, they definitely wanted to talk about their health issues, not about making improvements. Unquestionably a moaning session, four people gave their time and we listened. I do hope it was of value to them.

Our claim to fame, the consultants' event, we emailed

invites and prepared the post graduate auditorium. The room holds about eighty comfortably sat. We filled the room with almost a hundred consultants, unheard of at one event. The best attendance numbers by far.

Many engagement sessions had a topic related to improving communication in one form or another. In collaboration with Haelo, (an innovation and improvement science team who helped tackle challenges in Health and Social Care) I supported a physiotherapist. His mission was to improve communication for a specific group of patients, on discharge from hospital. The cohort for these missions were spread throughout the North West, we met monthly at the Lowry in Manchester. Large tables filled the room with groups from many different hospitals all with different missions to bring about change.

At first, we had a full team of eight attending. We had a couple of physios, me, a respiratory consultant and others from our Trust. The Haelo team really inspired me, it was the first time I had met them and remember feeling I could learn something here. I was really keen I always am when it comes to change. By the end of the second session, I realised the others were not as enthusiastic about continuing. I don't know what happened but they lost interest? Both me and the physiotherapist went to the sessions held each month, however, at the last hurdle he was unable to make it and I sat alone at our hospital table.

The physiotherapist was successful and received acknowledgment from the Haelo team. I thoroughly enjoyed all the presentations provided by this company. The last training session I attended with them was in 2017, I should have graduated from the improvement science for leaders IS4L programme, which is a yearlong course that supports teams to develop and sustain improvements. Unfortunately, I missed the last couple of sessions.

This role introduced me to many members of staff, I recall fantastic sessions and conversations with Glynis (head of security) and the police officers, radiology, ENT, lots of wards and A&E, secretaries, ward clerks, payroll and the consultants too many to mention.

We travelled quite a bit to join other Trusts across England to learn from their experiences. The only journey I can really recall was to Oxford. We met at Manchester Piccadilly station to get the early train. We took different members of the sponsor groups to spread the learning.

I arrived early at the station and bought a coffee while waiting for others to arrive. Ann one of the nurses met me and we waited for Julie and a couple of consultants. I forgot to check the board and our platform number changed. Five minutes to go, I said "we better make our way to the platform" the phone rang. It was Julie "where are you". The train had left the station without us.

We had a chat with one of the clerks at the station, if we took two trains, we would catch the group in Birmingham, continuing to Oxford together. I had my ticket and Ann purchased one to Birmingham. Our train was leaving in two minutes, I needed the toilet. Ah it will be Ok, there will be a toilet at the next stop.

We arrived at the station and asked the guard which platform the Birmingham train was leaving from, he said "that's your train you better run". Up the stairs and down to another platform we jumped on the packed train. People were sat on the floor in the aisles and in doorways. I couldn't have used the toilet even if I could have found it, there were just too many people. The whole journey was spent in concentration, not wetting myself.

The train pulled into Birmingham, I saw Julie and the others, Ann joined them. I spotted a toilet sign and ran into the nearest cubicle and started peeing. I couldn't stop, it was such a relief. I deciding if I miss the next train, I was going to go home it just wasn't my day. It took ages to empty my bladder. On leaving the cubicle and washing my hands I noticed a man standing on the other side of a window, mouthing "madam you're in the gents". Ah well, I didn't care, my bladder was empty and the men at the urinals didn't turn round. I caught the train. I thought the loos smelt

273

a bit whiffy.

It was around this time I joined Mikes army and applied to be a specialist advisor for the Care Quality Commission (CQC). Sending a short resume wasn't easy, there was so much I wanted to say. They interviewed me and a telephone call confirmed my success. They were looking forward to working with me. I was contemplating another new challenge.

The first inspection took five days and the group stayed at a local hotel. The rooms were fine but the food wasn't the best. That seemed to be the standard for all the inspections I did, hotel rooms good, food requires improvement. At one inspection we had to order takeaway pizza as the offerings at the hotel were so poor.

During the first day we sat in inspection groups, maternity, A&E, theatres etc., we talked about information required by inspectors for inclusion in their reports. There was no induction for me, you went with the flow and learned on the job. Quite normal in the NHS I call it being a self-starter.

We left early the following morning travelling to the hospital site by coach. We parked on the main road in the hospital grounds. The Trust representative met the inspection team and directed us to our base for the week. We had coffee, gathered our thoughts and left with our warrants and identification to begin our information gathering.

On inspections you carry a warrant and passport to identify yourself to anyone who asks. My first task was to meet a department manager and discuss her team. A jittery shaking woman opened the office door she appeared shocked by my arrival. I felt awful, and asked if we could just sit and chat for a while.

"Do you need to call anyone" she seemed relieved and rang her manager to warn them.

"The CQC are in the department".

It wasn't an unannounced inspection, we were expected. She settled down and we went through a list of questions I had put together. I was gathering information on how the department functions. This was my first inspection. There wasn't anyone to check if I was good enough to be doing this role. Were the questions I asked getting the information the inspectors required. All a little unnerving for me but I was doing my best for the CQC and for that manager. I did a lot of prompting. As a department manager, I knew how difficult it is when put on the spot, to have the correct information to hand.

My opinion at the time was the hospital knew we were arriving and she should have been a little prepared. I remember asking about patient safety and the incident and complaints book with action plans and progress. I was shocked to hear that they hadn't had an incident or complaint for such a long time. That rang alarm bells for me and I made a note on my pad.

For some reason she had not thought about the very basic requirements of inspections, prove how you are safe, effective, caring and responsive. She gave a good response to questions about leadership in her department though. Hmmm.

She showed me round the area she was responsible for and we discussed a couple of issues. The morning flew by, I felt our meeting was successful, we stopped for lunch. I was a little unsure of the conversations I was hearing back at the base room. Many of the specialist advisers were retired and might not be current, some advisors focused and sought anything that wasn't perfect. Everyone worked through lunch writing up their experience of the areas they had been inspecting.

In the evening, back at the hotel we sat before our evening meal discussing the findings of the day. They got their monies worth out of the specialist advisors; it was none stop from 8:30am to 8pm. I raised my concerns with the inspection leader. Her response to my thoughts were "keep doing inspections and question everything and everyone, don't stop working for the CQC we need to make improvements to our service too, if we are not challenged, we won't get the inspections right". I felt she understood, I was happy with her response. She gave me a list of questions, she used when inspecting hospitals, she hoped it would be useful to me. It was.

276

I met wonderful caring staff on these visits and began to realise in many hospitals the environment is poor the equipment and furniture old and staff are worn out.

During every inspection the CQC hold open forums for hospital staff. They are run by two of the inspection team, I ran one of these sessions. I remember listening firstly to complaints about managers being present, preventing staff from speaking freely. A couple of managers left the room. I listened and documented what was said and handed all the information to the inspector for them to address in their report. I couldn't give advice even though I had heard it all before, my role wasn't to advise, but to listen and document. I couldn't use my mediation skills or give them advice about responding to bullies or using reporting mechanisms to gain some control over the situation they found themselves in.

At one unannounced inspection my role was to look at an out-patient's clinic. Most things looked fine, but as the day moved on, I began to notice over run clinics with patients sat on the floor. At another clinic there were a handful of patients. I questioned both lists with the nurse. They considered the number of patients attending that day as normal for those consultants. Saying "his clinic is always very busy and patients wait for such a long time to be seen and the other clinic is finished in just over an hour". The nurse complained that staff on the quiet clinic wouldn't help those on the busy clinic. What had happened to the template for booking these clinics, when were they last updated? How did the directorates feel about these clinics? That was for the next day.

I took a walk and found a long corridor where a respiratory clinic was being run. There was a small reception desk and seating for about six people which were all occupied. Patients were standing, one man on oxygen was sat in his wheelchair. I spoke to the patients then went to find a member of staff. My main concern the patient using oxygen was still attached to his portable cylinder not the hospital supply and portable cylinders don't last very long. A physiotherapist changed the supply. I felt this wasn't normal practice. Another note for the pad.

The next day I took a taxi to visit the building where clinic bookings were processed. I was back at a spreadsheet, database target driven workplace. I was trying to get my head around why the clinics were running overbooked against others that were underutilised. The office was a nicer building than the outpatient clinic patients attended. This was an unannounced visit but once the CQC arrive at a hospital the grape vine will inform everyone in the building very quickly. When a member of the CQC team want to look into an issue a little deeper the inspection lead contacts the Trust and arrangements are made for the inspectors and/or advisors to visit and discuss the issue with the specific department.

The department were expecting me and the clerks were aware of my concerns and we discussed their processes. They couldn't have been more helpful. The department was well run and I was reminded of my own team back at Booking and Scheduling, it was like old times. A meeting was arranged for me to speak to one of the Directors and my concerns were listened too. I was more confident now and hope the issue was sorted out.

Over the next couple of years, I continued working with sponsor groups and doing inspections for the CQC. I worked on unannounced and announced inspections at hospitals in London, Birmingham and Leeds. In my heart I don't believe these inspections work to improve quality, they seem such a waste of time and money. I agree they do highlight very poor care; I believe the staff already know this and for some reason feel unable to report it or make changes themselves. Is it a lack of knowledge, finance, or have they become so jaded and detached emotionally that they do not recognise poor care?

If a Trust needs improvement hasn't it already failed and putting a label on it won't make it change. Costly inspections don't bring about permanent change. Increasing the number of nurses may have a better impact on quality. Inspections can be demoralising and addressing the root cause of problems may be a better choice. It is often those on the front line that have to increase their work load to meet the demands of inspectors. Mix it up, interhospital transfers of staff, experience how others work. Witnessing different approaches and attitudes to care may bring about change at some level.

Earlier I spoke about a blame culture and all these years later nothing has changed. Why does the NHS think a blame culture approach will bring about a positive change and improve quality? When I joined the CQC I thought I would be able to make a difference, using my experience to support teams with ideas and tools I have used over the years. I realised the inspections created a fear environment, a reflection of the state of the hospitals. Staff are definitely afraid. Telling the truth that no one really wants to hear is difficult.

Bad things happen to people that whistle blow. Employees disappear, all NHS staff have experienced this. You could be labelled, your card marked, lose your job, be bullied or ostracised. A colleague simply disappears and their name is spoken in whispers. You spoke every day for years they never mentioned leaving or even thinking of moving on, yet one day they are gone.

A new CEO arrived at our Trust; she wasn't interested in what we had been doing. She wasn't interested in our successes. We all know what happens when new seniors or executives arrive at a Trust, your colleagues begin to disappear, one after another, sometimes in groups, they're gone. Senior staff bring their own team. They come as a package and are all on the same journey, the CEOs journey. It doesn't matter if the new broom swept out experienced or skilled staff. All that seems to matter is the new boss gets exactly what they want, with the people they have built working relationships with. Changes were happening at a rapid rate for many in senior positions. New faces were appearing on the executive floor every day.

While I was on annual leave, Julie and Lynn had a visit from a woman who would be joining the Trust at a later date, after her maternity leave. She would be joining as the Director of Quality Improvement and managing our team was part of her role. Julie wasn't keen and found herself a new position in the project management office (PMO) at Crumpsall my mother ship. I was sorry to see Julie go she is one of the most generous people I have worked with, always thinking of her staff and buying lunch and little gifts when out and about. What a kind generous woman. Good manager but I imagine she could be tough too.

My promotion to LiA lead followed, I was one point from the top of a band seven now and happy with that wage, it was enough. Lynn and I continued with the conversations and providing support to the sponsor groups. The months passed by, I felt lucky to be in a happy place at work with Lynne.

In the interim period between Julie leaving and the new boss arriving, I used my new mediation skills with a couple of large teams and individuals with bullying problems. You listen when mediating often to disagreement about a work issue or someone's attitude. Getting two people or sides to move on past a disagreement can be difficult. We have to be professional but it was often the one being bullied that made the adjustments not the bully, so wrong.

The approach we were taking was working. We provided the support and the teams came up with the innovative ideas to achieve positive outcomes, all flowing from the initial pulse check. This bottom-up approach worked and I loved this role but knew things were changing too. The LiA approach was being phased out and something else would take its place. But what.

Verandern rapid process improvement was waiting in the wings. There was nothing wrong with LiA or Veranderns approach to change. They had different methods and tools to achieve positive change and outcomes. Everything depended on which CEO was at the helm. The poor staff on the shop floor were fed up of, do it this way. No, do it that way. No, we have changed again it should be this way.

We had over a hundred LiA sessions and many successful outcomes. The most impact came from being out there, being seen, being approachable, that's where success was.

We provided encouragement and mentorship; we were accepted as improvement leaders and were making a difference. Our time was devoted to making things better for staff and patients, simply by engagement, visiting the workplace and chatting. We even sold raffle tickets for a car to engage with staff. It was our mission to be approachable and it had worked.

One day while Lynn was typing notes from an LiA session our new boss arrived, she was very friendly. We had coffee and discussed her expectations and vision for the future. She wanted Lynn and me to move to Crumpsall Hospital, Trust HQ my mother ship. I was happy to work at any site but Lynn wanted to stay put. Within the week the boss was back telling us to pack up and move to the project management office (PMO).

She described where we would be sitting and left us to it. I suppose we could have eked it out for a week or so but like ripping a plaster off a wound we decided to pack up. We were to take all but the desks, we packed computers, printers, chairs and files. The new boss hadn't realised how efficient we were and a couple of hours later we had boxes delivered and were packed ready to leave. It was a sad time leaving Fairfield with its wonderful staff. I was returning to the mother ship and the staff who said hello every morning with a nod and a smile as we passed on the corridors.

A couple of months before we moved out of Fairfield, I received a call from my sister, mum had been seen in an outpatient clinic South of Manchester and needed admitting to hospital. The outpatient nurse waited with mum but the ambulance didn't turn up. She decided to take my mum to hospital herself with the help of her husband, how she managed to get her in the car I will never know, she requires a hoist for her transfers. My sister rang because she had been unable to find where mum had been taken. I rang round the hospitals she wasn't at any that I called. I was getting worried and eventually rang an on-call manager and asked for help, she was great and found my mum a while later sat in a wheelchair in the corner of an A&E department. She was wet and the staff had put paper hand towels between her legs to soak up the urine. Disgraceful. She was sat there alone.

Very sad, and they call that care. Mum wasn't in the best of health; she was blind and partially deaf riddled with rheumatoid arthritis and totally dependent on carers. Now she was wet and in a strange environment with sounds she couldn't identify. Imagine how scared she must have been. Mum was admitted to the medical assessment unit and we stayed on the unit until she was asleep. That was my mother ship, I cried.

I returned on the Saturday morning to check she was

Ok after the extremely stressful day she had experienced. Mum had been moved to one of the medical wards. I set off walking down the corridor remembering the smells of the building and greeting the many faces as I walked along, auto pilot took me to the doctor's mess and the doors were open, I strolled through passing my old office, it looked just the same really.

Another desk and more PCs had been added and the juniors were using the room as a resource area. I arrived at the entrance to the ward, hoping the staff would be OK with me visiting early, it was around ten o'clock.
Most staff were sat in the office having coffee and toast, the ward manager greeted me with:
"What are you doing here Moira" "I'm here to visit my mum" "Who's your mum"
"Sheila Rothwell"

The ward manager stood up and grabbed mums notes from the trolley, as she opened the folder all the admitting loose papers shot across the office with a do not resuscitate (DNR) form landing at my feet. The ward manager said,

"I assume you know about that" "No, I didn't, but do now"

That DNR wasn't discussed with the family, how rude to write a loved one off without even speaking to a family member and we had sat in her room on her admitting ward for hours. There was no excuse.

I went on the ward to find mum, she was OK but needed the toilet, one nurse with a cardboard bed pan went behind the curtain and tried to get mum from a lying position to roll onto the pan. There was no way mum would be able to do that and I asked if they had a hoist, the response was "we don't use hoists on this ward". You just cannot believe the things I overheard and witnessed; a catalogue of uncaring acts and comments began to occur: - scanning the wrong leg, not using hoists, continually putting hospital nighties on mum that were too tight and marked her skin, when her own night wear was in the cupboard, fluid and food charts were never filled in properly, was she starved and dehydrated? I visited twice a day and I cannot say I ever witnessed mum being fed or given a drink.

Those were my witnessed complaints; my sister had another list. I was concerned that mum wasn't getting enough to drink and the water I gave her just wasn't enough to sustain anyone. I spoke to four specialist nurses that worked at the hospital; I was wondering if they would allow their mum to be cared for on that ward, the response was a firm "no" from all but one of them. I was ashamed and disgusted, how can senior nurses say that, why haven't they done something about it, why does it have to be left to family to complain about these issues.

The complaint letters were many pages long and

every day either me or my sister added to them. I remember sitting next to mum when the consultant (who I knew) did his round and he told me to get her home she will be better off there. How bad is that. Both me and my sister (a specialist nurse) put in a large complaint about the poor care on that ward and that complaint has never been closed, as far as we are concerned, her care was inadequate and they didn't respond to the complaint correctly. That same day I asked one of the nurses to let me know as soon as mum was discharged. I followed the ambulance and asked the nurse where she lived to do a full check of her skin, she had a small pressure sore on her bottom that wasn't there before. It was written in her notes that under no circumstances must she be allowed to return to that hospital and she wasn't.

Spring bank holiday mum passed away. She always said she wanted to come to one last party at my house and she sort of did.

The hearse arrived and I opened the side gates and watched the men carry mum in her coffin to the patio doors at the back of our house. There were two steep steps into the lounge and I had to help the men with the coffin, which was placed on a stand in front of my fire. After the undertakers left, I sat for a while just staring at the coffin, I cannot describe how I felt, then I lay down on the couch.

Three hours later I woke, probably the first good sleep I'd had since mum died. When I woke the house was quiet and still, Mum spent the night and family sat with her for her last party. We drank tea and had a glass of wine while we remembered her. My sisters stayed over and my niece brought her daughter, it was the first time we had seen her but unfortunately, she didn't settle and spent most of the evening crying, they left earlier than they probably wanted to. Mum had a fantastic send-off which she thoroughly deserved and was laid to rest in Urmston cemetery.

The next time I saw the manager from the ward mum was on, she had been promoted to a specialist nurse and was attending one of the LiA conversations.

That same year my mother-in-law Janet took ill and was admitted to a medical ward at my mother ship. She was in for a couple of weeks, our first visit went well, everything seemed fine she was being looked after and appeared to be improving. The second time we visited two days later, she complained that doctors were getting on her nerve. An eighty-year-old woman complaining about doctors, rare. Janet was the type of person that considered doctors as God like and she was complaining, something was wrong.

"What's the matter Janet"
"The doctors keep asking me about my drugs. I can only remember the medication for my shingles and those after my heart bypass".

"That's OK that's all you have taken". "Now, they

want me to have a HIV test" "Go on, you're kidding" Laughing "What did you say"

"I have only had one sexual partner and that was Harry" "Ah, Janet it's OK I will sort this out".

Janet was obviously upset. I spoke to the nurse, I knew her, and asked why the doctors wanted her to have a HIV test. She laughed too. We went to look at Janet's notes. Without my glasses I couldn't see anything documented. The nurse started to read, then snapped shut the notes. She informing me consent was required from Janet to allow her speak to me. I collected my glasses, what on earth is documented in her notes. Her notes read:

PC/ (Presenting Complaint): SOB (shortness of breath) PMH/ (Past medical history) IV (intravenous) drug user, Heroin addict, abscesses.

Nothing about her triple bypass for which she has a scar, nothing about her shingles which had caused her pain for years. I knew what had happened, but couldn't understand why so many highly qualified experienced staff (consultants, SHOs, HOs, nurses and physios) didn't use their brains and ask Janet what her scar was from and what her main complaints were. That would have identified the wrong set of notes. My friend Jackie worked on that ward and knew what had been documented, but patient confidentiality prevented her from mentioning it to me.

After explaining to Janet, there was a mix up with notes, she settled. Her children (my husband and his brother) started to wind her up, "so that's why we didn't have good shoes or clothes because you were buying drugs", she had a good sense of humour. This shouldn't have happened; she had been an inpatient for too long for this sort of error to have continued. She took it well, but an eighty-year-old shouldn't be upset telling her daughter in law she has only had one sexual partner. That just isn't good enough.

How many times is it now that something not quite right has happened with the care of one of my family.

The next day I email the CEO, "you won't believe this" and told my story. I was contacted that evening and asked to pop on the ward the next day for a chat. I was happy to attend. I arrived at the ward and was taken into the office. Two consultants and the ward manager were waiting for me. I knew them all. One consultant started with:

"Moira I'm really sorry this happened, if it had been one of the usual dick heads, I could understand, but it wasn't. A really good junior made the mistake".

Who did the consultant think he was talking too? Calling doctors dick heads to a member of a patient's family? I knew this consultant, but come on, where was his professionalism. No mention that Janet had been on the ward for days and not one member of staff had worked out they were using a much younger patients notes with completely different complaints, past medical history and diagnosis. I asked had anyone spoken to Janet and apologised, they reassured me that happened earlier. The consultant handed me a small stack of loose notes taken from the medical records. My response was "I don't want them" the consultant said I will shred them then. Legal document and all that.

No comment.

You just cannot make this up. Why didn't he just cross through the notes and write written in error then add the information in Janet's correct medical records.

Janet returned to the hospital in the October her final hospital stay. She was on a respiratory ward and received exceptional care from the nursing and medical staff. She had a gentle death drifting away while sleeping, surrounded by her sons and daughters in law and a couple of her grandchildren. We lost both our mums within months of each other. Sad times.

I just want to say I worked at the hospital for over thirty years and although it let my family down at times, it also provided some of the best care and understanding at others. Don't judge the hospital so harshly, I have written more letters of gratitude to NMGH than I have complaints so don't be afraid of using it as your hospital, I do.

Recently in 2024 Vin was very sick and nearly died from covid. I wrote to acknowledge that all my confidence in the hospital has been restored as I couldn't fault them in A&E, Radiology, Medical doctors and nurses and especially the care given by the Infectious Diseases team.

WARRIORS

Lynn and I arrived at our new workplace parking our cars outside the basement of Trust Headquarters. I knew we could access a lift to the PMO from there. The area at the entrance to the lift was usually full of rubbish that's blown in on the swirl of wind rotating around the door. In the winter, the rubbish builds up blocking the drain, creating a pool of water deeper than your shoes, making the entrance unusable. As you open the door, you see the ancient metal hand rail of the stone staircase, all worn and paint less. There were usually boxes stored alongside the stairs and I wondered what Lynn was thinking about her new place of work. We had left an office in a well-presented building that was painted and clean looking, here it looked old and uncared for.

We sourced two large metal cages on wheels to transport our equipment and easily filled them with computers, printers and chairs. Lynn wasn't happy, I could see it in her face. I did my best to reassure her, it would be OK.

We rattled our way with full cages into the PMO, as the cages came to rest, we looked around not one smiling face. We weren't greeted by any of the staff.

Oh dear, not welcome. You know that feeling when you walk into the wrong door, disturbing a speaker and the audience turn to stare at you. Well, it was the right door but the faces weren't saying that, I would even use the word, hostile. One of the staff made a dash for the door, obviously going to complain, that two strangers had moved themselves into the department.

I kept smiling at Lynn to reassure her but it was difficult, we weren't comfortable. We had left a professional friendly happy office with a real can-do attitude. To an old dirty looking building where no one smiled. The office occupants hadn't been told of our arrival; a smile wouldn't have gone a miss though. My first impression, awful.

A woman was using the desk space I was told to use, thankfully without too much discussion, she moved her lap top to one of the other vacant desks allowing me and Lynn to install our PC's printer and phones while crawling around on our hands and knees. I was joining Lynn in her OMG what have we come to state. We notified our new manager of our arrival. On returning to the office the printer had been moved and without a welcome my hackles were spiking.

"Who's moved my stuff" I asked. The woman sat opposite me pointed to the IT man in the back office. She didn't say much and did her best to avoid eye contact, she pointed to the door "the IT man".

I went into the office behind my desk and asked him why he moved the printer. He pointed to the woman opposite me "she told me to move it".

Was she the office manager having final say where equipment was located? No. The office spaces were booths with sides, I couldn't understand why she needed to move anything I was opposite her with a solid screen separating the two workspaces. I didn't raise my voice it's loud enough; I wasn't rude. I wasn't in her space, why did she feel she was allowed to move things around. She said the printer noise would annoy her.

You could feel the tension in the room but I was here to work and that was what I did. The woman opposite me disappeared for a while obviously moaning to her boss. Keep your cool and smile, I felt my short fuse had been lit, me and Lynn sat there feeling totally unwanted.

The call came for me to go to the manager's office where I watched the smirk on the face of the woman who sat opposite me. She was loving this and the disagreement voiced by her had been manipulated. She was part of our team, how welcoming is that. My initial thoughts were, they are either friends or the manager needs her. The woman didn't have to speak because the manager did it all and basically turned everything onto me.

"Moira the PMO is a very professional office and there

will be very little speaking, you mustn't raise your voice, people are trying to concentrate". She didn't know that office at all, was I the one that would have to educate her on the state of not only the environment but the unfriendly occupants and the miss information that she would be receiving too.

Lesson one learned, my new manager has favourites and doesn't listen to the truth, she takes sides. I apologised, did the woman opposite me apologise for moving my things. No. I always apologise and throughout my career I've taken the blame when Junior doctors have forgotten to do something, when clerks sent out the wrong information, I'm always happy to apologise or take the blame, it can make life easier. My apology may even fulfil a persons need to feel superior, that's OK, superiority isn't something I sought. Their Karma not mine, I believe in what you do, your intent, your actions may impact on another individual and their future. You must judge yourself on how you treat others and bad judgements and decisions often come back to bite you.

Lynn was called to the manager's office later that day. She was concerned about the meeting and her role in this new department, I was beginning to feel the same. When you're not made welcome it's very difficult to see past the moment. Lynn discovered she would be returning to a secretarial support type position and further opportunities may follow later. When she arrived back at her desk, she was upset and unimpressed. The boss told Lynne to be her eyes and ears in the office. A spy in the camp, and to report what she was witnessing back to the her. Lynn didn't like this at all, the new manager put her in a position that no employee should be asked, to spy on her colleagues.

Lesson two, the boss thinks it's OK to spy on her staff. My initial thought was the new boss mustn't be confident in her team, but who are her team. Me and Lynn and the woman opposite, not sure. The day was over and nobody had introduced themselves. I suppose I could have introduced myself around the offices that formed the PMO but that should have been arranged. Let it go, its day one and so far, me and Lynn hadn't seen one smile or welcome, and I was already apologising for being me. Disgraceful.

I soon settled into this new environment because I loved the work but Lynn struggled from day one. She disliked her new role. I often wondered if it was just too far from home or if it was being a spy in the camp. She struggled for a while and I did my best to involve her in as much as I could. It made me sad watching her new skills being pushed to the side. Our new manager had no idea how much work and effort we had put into our roles. We relied on Lynn so much to support teams and sponsor groups. She was fantastic at preparing and organising; she was excellent at public speaking and had a fearless attitude to social events that I often floundered at. An honest loyal colleague and friend.

I soon picked up one person in the office wasn't very popular, and often heard something derogatory being whispered or sniggered in relation to her. I better get to know her then, not as a friend but I don't like people being excluded.

The situation took me back to my first year of high school and within the first month I fell ill and spent ten weeks in hospital. On return to school, I noticed one girl had been ostracised and I made friends with her. I had missed what had happened but knew she needed a friend, just like me.

I loved the work, just up my street. I wasn't concerned about popularity. My role was nothing to do with personality or sucking up to managers, which I was regularly witnessing. My work was always good and that was enough for now.

Within the project management offices there were four types of work, one group were involved in commissioning health care services for the Trust. Our team covered Quality Improvement; I cannot remember what the others did.

During one meeting the Director mentioned bad language in the office, I was thinking I bet she thinks it's me and Lynne (neither of us really swear). The boss had no idea what me and Lynn were listening to and I cannot remember who the people were that swore so much that it had been reported to the boss, I know it wasn't me or Lynn.

People talking incessantly about one upmanship, key sports for some in that department. How can she be a band 8b, what work does she do, she arrives late every day and goes early, she is senior and she didn't pass the course, she has to do it again. You had to be very careful here and I knew that on the first day, watch what you say and who you say it to.

The main thing about the people in this office environment, was their competitiveness and watching them compete with their colleagues for pay upgrades and even for ownership of ideas and solutions, became quite common. It was all about them and their need to demonstrate their superiority or knowledgeability.

Gossip was rife I'm surprised they hadn't heard we were moving in, someone slipped up there.

My poor memory for names was exposed here. I called Chris, Steve many times and occasionally he would give me this weird look. He never said anything. Then Steve, well I called him Peter and no matter how many times he corrected me and I corrected myself it stuck. He retaliated by calling me Mary and I always answered to Mary as well as Moira. It became a thing; I quite liked it. There was also a lot of similar names Amaara, Tamara, Samara and boy did that mess my head up.

The manager said awful things to me over the early months, "do you want to hand in your notice" "subdue your personality" amongst other things. She didn't like me, but I liked her. She kept me busy; she was a real educator. She didn't like criticism or being challenged and I did this too often for her to deal with. She kept me at a distance compared to others in the team. That was Ok I didn't expect her to be a friend. She always praised my work, that was good enough for me.

My LiA sponsor groups were completing their missions. I began to take on projects from the department. The first big piece of work related to nursing assessment and accreditation. The Trust were introducing this system so staff could focus on key risks to the delivery of care. My role was to organise the work that had been completed at other hospitals and establish which aspects could be used at our hospitals. We needed a system that measured the quality of nursing care, delivered by individuals and teams. There was a colour coded assessment that was awarded giving a timeframe for reassessing wards.

As the weeks went by my appraisal date came up and I expected very little from my new manager. My experience of appraisals had been very positive in this Trust but having a boss that didn't like me was going to be very different. I was wrong, she was OK, although her process wasn't standardised using the Trust format, she was pleased with my work and progress. I helped her out preparing and forwarding paperwork for use at her other appraisals she needed to use the Trust format and paperwork. She informed me an advertisement for a full-time person to take on my project was going out. Was I not good enough? I couldn't understand why she didn't just advertise for another quality improvement lead. Then I discovered the position would be for a higher band an 8a.

I completed and submitted my application but heard nothing else. I discovered the woman opposite me that created the atmosphere when we arrived at the office by moving my things shortlisted for the position, no wonder I didn't get an interview. I asked for feedback and my boss told me to speak to the person who was successful and compare our applications. How poor is that, I have never met a manager that couldn't give proper constructive feedback, she was a coward, my card was marked. I still liked her though; I know I'm stupid. Learning that a great review of your work in the NHS will not guarantee success is something I should have learned much earlier in my career.

I met with Amaara the lady taking over the work, we compared our applications. I learned nothing new really but Amaara asked could she use my wording in her future applications. She agreed with me I should have been interviewed as I easily met every aspect of the person specification. It was personal they hadn't followed the correct procedures, and I think that is so poor.

I began to pick up other projects and continued enjoying the work. The Trust were due to have a visit by the CQC and our team was growing. Vanessa a ward sister joined us; I had worked with her before on Listening into action. It was nice to see someone familiar and supportive.

Everyone with the exception of Amaara began wowing the wards for the CQC. The well organised ward (WOW) as it was called was a massive clean-up. Earlier I talked about the productive ward where I worked with Collette to get rid of rubbish and old stock plus tightening processes for the nurses.

Well, this was the same, we set off to our allocated wards and hospitals with porters and volunteers. Again, it was shocking witnessing the state of some areas, if you have ever seen the television programmes about hoarders, well, areas did actually look like that but without the filth. One door on a ward was hiding floor to ceiling feeds, another floor to ceiling bags of intravenous fluids, many out of date. One ward had bedding in the electricity cupboard. A sign on the door stated DO NOT OPEN DANGER OF DEATH.

We had to take photographs as we went along, proof of the poor conditions we witnessed. This wasn't an easy job; we ordered many cages to get rid of rubbish. New boards and large posters were ordered and all wards had to display specific information.

This was a big job; we weren't popular except at one ward, I did an initial inspection with the ward manager one of my old colleagues from the vascular ward, Heather. We both came to the conclusion the ward wasn't fit for purpose. For example, the toilet seat touched the partition wall, you couldn't sit properly, the wall was too close. In the next cubicle you couldn't reach the toilet roll unless you got off the toilet. The sink to wash your hands was in another room. Unbelievable. There was absolutely nowhere to store anything and that included fluids and medical equipment.

We moved the ward while alterations were completed. I made a list of actions from our inspection and passed the work list to teams that came along behind us. We inspected wards, cleared rubbish then plumbers, decorators and builders followed.

We had a fantastic female porter working with us to sort the wards out. Around this time Lynn began to look for another position and was successful in her application as a ward clerk nearer to her home.

I was very sad to see my friend leave.

We advertised for a new secretary. I was the only person with the training to chair an interview otherwise I wouldn't have been on the panel (which made me wonder if the interview for the 8a post was done correctly and who chaired the interview process).

This is where we picked up a wonderful woman who was confident at interview but not confident in herself and that stood out every day. She couldn't cope and told me many times that she didn't like being asked to spy on the team, it made her feel uncomfortable. I told her to only tell the boss what she was comfortable telling her and not to feel pressurised, it was an unrealistic request to a member of staff struggling to find their feet. All four teams of the PMO were excellent and supported our new lady which was really nice to see. She was definitely part of the whole office team not just a section of it. I blamed myself for not providing a better induction package which would have enabled her to learn at her pace, however I wasn't the manager of our team.

Walking down the main corridor one day, I was stopped by one of the matrons, we chatted for a while about one of the wards and a project I was working on. She seemed interested and I gave her as much information as I could. She could join the project if she wanted to help. Then it came, what she really stopped me for. Matron asked me to join her meetings to "sort her staff out".

She was having difficulty engaging with the ward managers and obviously didn't have any team building skills, very senior on the wards though. There was no way I was going to get involved there.

One area we went to wow was part of the new building and we experienced some badly organised stock rooms and a very bad-tempered manager. I remember watching a member of staff open the door to the stock room and throw a box in. When she moved away from the door, I looked inside the stockroom to find collapsed shelving and the floor covered in boxes and packages. That was my first job, organise that room and check the dates on everything. I ordered more shelving and a repair to the broken ones. Why this wasn't done before, I have no idea.

Now I was wasting all those years of education, learning how to manage, lead and build teams to organise stock and clear rubbish. Not that it was beneath me but what a waste of resources. The whole team did this all band 7 or above including the Director, the cost of preparing for the CQC. The final straw on that ward happened when a member of our team found mouse droppings in a cupboard. These cupboards allowed access from the patients' room and the corridor, they usually contained bedding and equipment for use in the individual rooms.

We found cups and drinking material including sugar and coffee. The mouse droppings were coffee and sugar that had soaked up spilled liquid. What was wrong with the kitchen cupboards, I have no idea. The manager wasn't happy and had a proper go at me and the team. She was quite threatening, I didn't join her outburst, I was really pleased with myself. I stayed calm which I think made her worse she was angry and shouting abuse at us. She ended her explosion with:

"I'm going to put in a complaint to the chief executive about your team and particularly you"
I did respond to that I said, "Go on then"

I later refused to return to her ward until she apologised. May be, it's my age but I was getting fed up of being treated badly in this new role. The next thing, my manager asked to speak to me about a complaint from a ward sister. Guess what her opinion was. "Moira you have to tread carefully in these circumstances". I was furious and told the manager to speak to others that were present. Her response was, "Think how much stress the ward manager is under, let's leave it there for now, we don't want to ruffle any feathers". A manager in denial. I didn't go back to that ward. There are just too many managers in denial in the NHS, was I the only one meeting them.

There was definitely a new language to learn in this job, our diaries were getting full with meetings and projects and after attending a couple of these, I realised buzz word bingo, would be a great game to play. There was no mention of patients or nurses and many meetings had such a poor diversity of thought. You heard it in one meeting and again in another and another. The main buzz word which I hated to hear was resilience. I can honestly say I only ever heard the word resilience a couple of times, that is until I began working with one of the quality improvement team, she used the word every other sentence. I began to dislike it so much I did my utmost not to use it.

Our new CEO was a fan of rapid process improvements and hired a company called Verandern to help our Trust learn about reducing waste. She had worked with them before and our role would be to pass on the knowledge, by training staff in the same way we were going to be trained, through workshops. The learning brought together our team and staff from the shop floor to improve a process. The company (Ian and Laura) facilitated the workshops to help accelerate the changes we required. We were looking at improving the processes by reducing time, wait, energy and resources.

The workshops were very educational and I really appreciated the time and effort the company put in to get everyone to understand the complexities of using new tools that identified waste.

One CEO liked a bottom-up approach using LIA, our next CEO liked Rapid improvements top-down approach. I can say that the last manager I had didn't like rapid change. Roundabouts. Do we ever get it right?

Our quality improvement team were lucky in a job that provided excellent training and time for learning. We were growing and Nadine came to join us, I had worked with her before, in fact she had been my boss at one point. I did two pieces of work for her when she was managing a couple of Directorates. She had held very senior positions in the Trust and had a vast amount of experience of the shop floor. She sat next to me and I was pleased to see another familiar face, I didn't have to watch what I said too.

Then two young women joined us from the graduate scheme, Natasha and Sarah, they were so enthusiastic and full of energy it was like working with the Junior doctors again. Our second admin person left and Alison came to join us from A&E. There were seven quality improvement leads now all on different pay grades, all doing the same work and one co-ordinator and the Director, nine in total. A doctor joined our team at one point, he had been put on some sort of gardening leave, but our boss was happy to have him in the department to help. I have no idea why he was on this kind of leave. One day while I was out and about, a couple of the Directors came into the office and he was asked to leave. The rumour mill set off, people in that department had access to many systems that held very personal information about staff including court hearing results. Hmmmm, wonder what happened there.

In my opinion Nadine was the most senior and professional of the whole team you could see it. However other team members wouldn't accept this view as it would affect their perceived image of themselves.

The conversations around pay and workload became a real issue, one of the team talked the Director into giving her a band 8b. In my opinion that was wrong, we had four band 7s and 3 band 8s all doing the same job. Inequality at its best.

I had an issue with the graduates starting mid-way up a band 7 when it had taken me years to get there, I understood the girl's opinion, we were doing the same job but my thought was they should have started at the bottom of a band 7. To be honest, they were good at their job and yes probably deserved their pay.

The Director was wrong she should have cleared the pay problem right at the beginning of her appointment. Quality Improvement Leads on two pay bands in the NHS in the same room and building doing the same work. Not on.

Now, the office atmosphere was palpable with gossip and vitriol from some. "What does she do differently to the others to deserve the pay increase, she's not an 8b" "Was the job advertised" they checked. "What has she got over the Director" "No way is she that level" "Its fixed", "let's ring recruitment to see how long the advert was live for".

I banged my drum for the band 7s but the boss wasn't listening. Sarah said I was the only one that tried to make her understand how we felt. I was grateful to Sarah for acknowledging that, but as I said earlier our boss wouldn't respond well to any challenge or criticism.

The whole purpose for some members in that office seems to be self-promotion, trying to advance their own career by giving an impression that everything was good. Anything that jeopardises that was a threat and dealt with in quite a hostile way. You can always see the favourites because they will display the very same characteristics so that they can survive.

I reckon if the team read this book, they will be a little shocked at my thoughts, but they are all true I'm being honest and a couple of them won't like it, I was always honest.

What was different about our team related to information moving up. Our team manager knew everything that happened in that office. Our team and in particular, a couple of the team kept her up to date on every conversation or discussion from the office and not just from our group. The manager would be able to stay in denial because these were unofficial lines of communication. I knew she knew everything going on in that office including how distasteful we all felt it was to promote one member of the group at the expense of all the others.

The boss one meeting mentioned basing herself in the office, I wish she had, she needed to. She would have witnessed members of the office with such good knowledge of the Trust and the type of staff working in it. She would have witnessed how productive and adaptable some members were and staff motivated massively to improve their skills and creativity. Instead, she didn't trust many staff and she ignored our workplace conflict which is a critical responsibility of a leader. Denying conflict, ultimately destroys trust and builds resentment.

We were spending too much time firefighting, concentrating on mainly short-term problems. I felt we were neglecting the long-term issues that we could plan for. This was a very top-down approach to quality improvement and I don't think that always works. There was quite a bit of friction in our group at times, not so much the other teams. However, we were fantastic grafters, we allowed for our differences of opinion and outspokenness, possibly mainly my outspokenness. On more than one occasion I was asked to take over the work of a band 8. The projects weren't moving forward and there was a problem. On one of the occasions, the band 8 could overhear what the Director was saying to me. She sat watching our manager asking me to take over her project, there was a problem with the work moving forward. I remember looking at her as the boss was talking. Not on, this should have been done privately. My boss knew I was capable of doing the work and thought it was OK to give a band 7, the work of a band 8 when another band 8 could have taken it on. In fact, post my retirement I met the band 8 and she confirmed she was aware the director gave me her work.

When I managed teams there were no circumstances where I would tell one team member that another's work wasn't good enough. Sad really.

One of our team members mentioned to me on numerous occasions that she felt excluded, she will never come forward and talk about this, so learning will never happen, but the Director ignored the most professional most experienced member of our team in such a way that she felt excluded.

Where had my laughter gone again, that giggling had waned, my spirit was ebbing, I'm not surprised with the things my boss said to me.

What are you to do just carry on? She even mentioned spending her weekend speaking to ACAS and asked me if I was keeping a diary of the inappropriate things, she was saying to me. Well, I was keeping notes for this book, not a diary, still I didn't lie.

I'm sure reading this you are thinking why did you stay. Well, I loved the work, anything that tries to improve quality of care is right up my street and I was used to managers moving on quite quickly. I loved the team even with our friction, you wouldn't think it but I did, every one of them had amazing skill and I learned from them all. They are nice women, hard workers and I appreciated them every day including the boss, and the woman that sat opposite me. I liked how visible the boss was she created time and space for the team to learn and do amazing things. I remember saying to the graduates, "you will never meet a boss like ours again in the NHS" and they probably won't. For all her management faults and the weird things, she said to me, she had a big heart and was generous with our family issues and important dates. She understood sickness and was flexible. So rare in the NHS. Looking back, my mood was low, I was stressed out and my emotions were all over the place. I'm surprised anyone in the office got out alive.

Caring had left its mark. I was worn out.

ANOTHER DIAGNOSIS

I took a day off work to take Vin for a kidney biopsy at one of the Manchester hospitals. I dropped him at the department and went to get my hair cut at my sisters' shop in Heaton Chapel "Helen Roberts". While having my hair done, I sat wondering what was happening to Vin, I waited for the call to pick him up. The call didn't come. I made my way back to the hospital and walked into the department. A doctor overheard me ask for Vin; she ran toward me.

"Who told you" Were her first words.
"Told me what" came my frightened response.

"I need to have a chat with you" she directed me to a chair at the side of the area. God, I was panicking what have they done to him? She was young and quite bothered in her manner, which didn't reassure me. "He's OK" she said, my face must have given away my thoughts. Vin had bled quite badly during the biopsy. Once they realised, he was bleeding they ran him to theatre and changed their minds on the way scanning him first.

The bleeding subsided slowly. He was OK but needed to be admitted. It could only happen to Vin. Apparently, the doctor informed him of the risks followed by, "but I have never had a problem". So, her first patient bleed. He was fine, and all I can remember about visiting him was the complaints about the food, so he must have been OK.

Since his transplant, Vin has suffered from many health problems some requiring procedures, skin graft for cancer, broken bones due to brittle bone disease caused by steroids, kidney and skin biopsies and treatment for cancers, too many things to list. He has had infections that required three months of home intravenous antibiotics. Our long sideboard became the clinical room to store boxes of equipment and medication. I used a white Ikea tray as a clean area to mix his antibiotics. I inserted and changed his cannulas and flushed his lines. Put his drips up and used an old metal coat hanger as a drip stand. Before work I would mix his antibiotics and connect his first bag, pop home at lunch to put up his second bag, the next bag was fine I was home from work. What we had to teach Vin to do, one handed, was disconnect his own drip and add a bung to stop any blood from his cannula.

Not one infection, we mastered it.

Today in lockdown because of Covid 19 he is waiting for yet another biopsy as a recent CT scan identified something on his bowel and kidney. We have to wait until the pandemic is over before he can get his biopsy and treatment.

He never complains and seems to have a happy disposition. People continue to comment on his health, "he looks so well" is always the default position. He does look well, but what they don't consider is what's going on inside. Do they think the comment "but you look good" will make him feel better, when he feels like his body is completely letting him down? You can look good but that doesn't mean you feel good. Vin always looks good and that makes it difficult for others to comprehend his limitations. I used to worry he didn't look sick enough and people wouldn't take his limitations seriously. I would limp when I got out of the car with a disability sticker on just to prevent any comments. If you find it hard to respond to Vins' list of conditions or limitations please don't default to "but you look good".

THE FINAL STRAW

Our days were busy and our boss began to call us "Warriors" I liked that too.

New description for my girls at home, Amazon Warriors.

Again, we were on the educational trail improving ourselves with access to a company called Aqua. The whole team participated in training on human factors, lean, patient safety and improvement practitioner. We were enrolled and completed a Prince2 project management course. With Haelo we enrolled on the IS4L leadership programme. I'm sorry for the nurses reading this, they just don't get the same opportunity, and it's wrong.

On the 11th August 2016 the CQC inspection results were published for my mother ship, they rated the services as inadequate. I wasn't surprised but very disappointed and a little broken hearted. The inspectors found services that were caring, but inadequate for being safe and well led. One site and community services were rated as good, one site required improvement and two sites were inadequate.

The report was very hard reading for me, I knew we were doomed, as a service we were the Quality Improvement Team and no matter how hard we had worked, some of the blame would fall on us.

I remember before the inspection talking about all top show and no substance with one of the clinicians. The hospitals had begun to look better, painted and repaired with new and professional posters. One of the smaller aspects of an inspection is the overall look of a hospital. They may make a comment on the appearance. Our Trust had spent too much time, money and energy trying to get the old decrepit building to look passable.

The nurses and doctors were fantastic, compassionate, caring and sensitive and the CQC could see they were understaffed. The serious concerns related to risk and the way the hospital was led. Our team were obviously very concerned.

I copied this from the report:

"Such is the level of concern that we have around quality and safety that in line with normal policy we would have considered recommending the trust should go into special measures. That would involve the appointment of an improvement director and supporting infrastructure which would assure CQC that the trust had the capacity to improve at pace. But we did have a Quality Improvement director my boss. Another Trust was asked to assume leadership immediately. Directors from Salford Royal took over the executive floor.

I was upset for the hospital and all its staff, a whole workforce demoralised by the negative word inadequate and it's written that same workforce are understaffed.

We have always known the mothership ran on good will and has done for so many years. In my heart, I knew the staff wouldn't be down for long they are the strongest most proactive and hardworking people I have ever met. Let's see what the new broom sweeps in were my thoughts. Most of our projects continued but the focus had changed. Everything was based around one large project with inspection findings as individual project within it.

My order of events won't be correct here there was too much going on, in my life. Our boss went on maternity leave, the changes were happening quickly on the executive floor. We discovered there would be a new Director of Quality, but what will be happening to the Director on maternity leave? Remember how staff just disappear. The team were introduced to the new Director of Improvement Siobhan, I wasn't around at this time and the team gave me quite a negative impression. My thoughts were, I will wait until I meet her and make my own mind up.

It was around this time our team began to visit departments and wards with the new executives, they needed to be seen. Our role was to show the Execs around the site and departments, introducing them to the wards. We were taking notes of the conversations and providing reports of the walkabout. With one of the execs, I visited orthopaedic theatres meeting the manager and a theatre nurse. The exec asked a list of questions and seemed to be getting positive feedback. These walkabouts were around the time of the Ariana Grande concert where a terrorist attack took place in Manchester, England, twenty-three people died and 1,017 were injured. Some of the injured were treated within the theatres at the mother ship. I asked the theatre staff how supported they felt during this time. "Not at all", came the response". if it hadn't been for one of the surgeons organising everything it would have been even more stressful". She mentioned how many hours they had been in theatre, I asked "did anyone come to thank you". She said "no". I hope that exec listened.

Vins health has often been somewhat up and down at this time, he was heading down. I would notice his difficulty walking and breathing all becoming more laboured and we had two wedding to attend on the calendar, which added to the stress.

My friend's daughter Hannah married Vinny her childhood sweetheart and the following week our son Paul was marrying Heidi his partner. We were looking forward to these special days. We had a wonderful day at Hannahs wedding and I can recall watching Karen her mum, proudly talking to all the guests.

The day after the wedding I received a phone call informing me Karen had fallen down a couple of steps in Manchester. She had been saying goodbye to wedding guests that were flying or driving back to Ireland when she lost her footing. An ambulance was called but her colleagues took a while to arrive, Karen worked for the ambulance service and answered our 999 emergency calls. She had a broken clavicle and would be going to theatre to have her bone pinned. I told her daughters I would visit after the weekend.

On Monday morning while on H4, I received a message my husband was trying to get hold of me. I knew it was Karen, she had died overnight. I drove home, picked Vin up and went straight to the hospital. Karen was in a side room, I walked in saying "your timing stinks Karen" as I kissed her forehead. Karen died because her oxygen saturations dropped and doctors did not respond to their bleep, nurses didn't chase the unanswered call, no follow up, amongst other issues.

I spoke to her nurse; she informed me Karen had broken her clavicle and would have gone to theatre to have the break pinned. The nurse also mentioned that Karen had banged her head during the fall, that fact had not been talked about, she informed me that a CT scan had been done on admission. I asked "had the scan been reported" the nurse went to check. She didn't come back to me because Karen had not had a scan and I don't think she banged her head during the fall. It was very sad, watching her girls (Karen has three daughters) they didn't want to leave their mum, eventually slowly they walked away.

I was bereft at the loss of my friend and with the pressure at work, the new broom and Vins deteriorating health, my thought turned to changing my hours. During this time my lovely colleague and friend Nadine was diagnosed with breast cancer and went on sick leave. Our team were dispersed across the Trust working at different sites. As the broom swept, you could see each individual become occupied with their own professional survival. The new manager deflected issues and concerns that were raised about pay and equality. Her denial and negativity were witnessed in individual meetings, nothing was said in public by this new broom. Nobody was listening, because nobody cared.

Our lovely hard-working team were finished.

The new broom swept in another level of management one based at each site, we would report to them. Danny was the person I now had to report to. I heard one of the new managers started to bully one of our team, she eventually became ill due to stress. Vanessa from the team met Siobhan and was told, "I don't want anything to do with nurses, you need to look elsewhere". I was so shocked, as far as I'm concerned there is no part of the NHS that can function without nurses.

The next thing I had to listen to was Danny telling me his previous role was as a car salesman. I wonder what he expected me to think?

The band 8b was definitely working her way into another position. Our team were leaving one by one. I made my decision to retire and work two days a week. I checked the policy and followed the correct procedure. I requested early retirement returning to a two-day week position making the two part time roles in the department, one whole time equivalent post. A job share position. The unions were very positive and told me it wouldn't be a problem. Managers need a really good reason not to support this sort of request when someone has caring issues.

I met Siobhan once, and that was in a group setting, but we hadn't spoken.

She asked could I travel to meet her at the executive offices in Salford Royal Hospital to discuss my retirement. According to policy, managers refusing a request to return to work post early retirement should write to the requester. The letter should offer a meeting to discuss options, with a reference to bring a union representative. If the request is going to be granted you do not require a letter. I had no letter. My thought was the meeting was to discuss which days I would be working and possible flexibility due to Nadine sickness.

I sat in the reception area waiting for Siobhan to arrive. She directed me to follow her into an office but before she even sat down, she said, "I'm not going to support your request; we cannot accommodate part time workers in this team". I was so shocked; My reply informed her that Nadine was part time, working three, seven and a half hour days. Siobhan was adamant she worked full time in three days, I knew then, she would lie her way out of any situation she found herself in. With me working two days a week the post would be a whole time equivalent. I thought I would give her the benefit of the doubt and asked if she had considered any other options for me. God, I was so wrong her strong reply was "No, I haven't given you or your retirement one thought". How awful. That new broom was appalling, talk about the psych bosses with no empathy well what can I say.

I was so shocked. She hadn't followed any kind of procedure. She was cold and callous to a person she didn't know. Imagine passing a stranger in the street one day, you nod acknowledging them. The second day you take away their income and force them into early retirement without a state pension and little chance of a two-day work opportunity to earn reasonable money. Why, because she could. Well, that is exactly what she did. I was absolutely fuming a red haze descended over me. She didn't even know me or ask who I cared for.

Absolutely shameful.

I was so restrained. I picked up my bag and left the room. I didn't like the way she made me feel. I walked out of the area and realised I had turned the wrong way, when I got to the door, she had to hold it open for me. I pointed at her, "Shame on you"!

I cannot type what I wanted to do to her I do not have the words and Vin would make me delete it anyway. Siobhan would not support a carer working two days a week in a job share with an employee working three days a week. Over thirty years of loyal service, all that knowledge and experience flushed down the pan in an instance.
Absolutely disgraceful.

The unions were of no help at all, and the information they gave me was wasted, but that's because they are spineless. Over thirty years paying union fees, what a waste of money? Do you think I could ask for a refund? I have never known a union rep at the mother ship that truly supported the workforce they were always definitely working for management.

I went home and visited my doctor; she wasn't surprised at all listening to my story. Many NHS staff require sick notes for stress because of callous heartless managers. My GP apologised for the poor managers that work in the NHS and gave me a sick note for three months. Time to grieve and time to care she said. I'm a great believer in what goes round comes around and I bet Siobhan has had bad times since we met, if not they will come.

I was angry not only at her but at myself for allowing her to affect me in such a strong manner, especially when I had so much to deal with at home. My anger subsided, eventually. I was still grieving for Karen and caring for my husband.

While my retirement was being processed the team had dispersed to different sites and roles at other Trusts. In March 2018 without even a card from that Trust my early retirement went through.

Nadine recovered enough to return to work without receiving a card or bunch of flowers from the new broom, in fact she didn't even contact her to see how her treatment was going. She works three days a week 22.5 hours, part time. Only in the NHS.

Back row: Me, Vanessa Beverley and Sarah
Front row: Alison, Amaara, Nadine and Natasha

My friend Karen and my sister Helen
at a hospital charity ball

As I mentioned before I read books written by NHS staff and I was sad to recognise so much within those pages, that it scared me. How much did I not report? How much did I walk past? How unsupportive was I? Did I challenge appropriately and enough? Probably not, it's that culture of assumption, I assumed when things went wrong and I reported them, something would be done.

My assumption now is nothing was done. When I reported the care at the Northern hospital, the care on the winter pressure ward, the phlebotomist for poor practice, the care staff for shouting at a patient, the bullying of a doctor and of other members of staff and the staff being too economical with the truth. When I complained about the care received by my family members and finally the story, I am unsure about mentioning. I have typed it and deleted it more than once, finally I removed the part I found difficult to tell you.

A handful of conversations, emails and documents had an impact on me emotionally. The most powerful one related to a telephone call asking me to print the contents of an email. The author of the email wanted to send a document as evidence relating to his/her suspension. I printed the document and read it. I was shocked to read a description of behaviour common in one of the departments witnessed daily by most staff. Shouting, swearing and blaming amongst other things. There was a descriptive event typed in great detail. The document related to a change in practice the results of findings from a never event. One person refused to comply with these changes and in temper behaved badly. I read this document to my manager, wanting to whistle blow the incident. I was reassured management were aware and the incident was being addressed.

I took no further action. Just before I started writing this book, I spoke to the manager who does not remember me talking about this incident. I went back to the author for confirmation and a little expansion. Everything and more were confirmed. I finally asked "was this reported as a serious incident". The response was "the incident was not reported".

Why did a whole team and multiple colleagues not report such a terrible incident? Why did they prevent an investigation? Why did my manager tell me it was being dealt with?

Deflecting issues when employees raise concerns seemed to be the go-to position for managers. Those in denial, do not listen and would not surround themselves with independent thinkers, that would be too much of a challenge. Managers in denial.

The general public think that if you work in the NHS, you get perks or special treatment, you don't. They think that the NHS provides a good place to work, it does for some, but not for all. Earlier I described the lack of flexible working, poor facilities and meagre access to training for nurses.

Everything in the NHS depends on who manages you, I met two managers that supported my caring needs. Most managers won't be aware of NHS England's approach and commitment to carers.

"Writing it down doesn't mean it happens" NHS England.

My experience of working in the NHS in relation to caring and carers relates to support or lack of it. The basics are not covered.

NHS England expects Trusts to be exemplary in its support of carers: -
It doesn't create a positive working environment for colleagues to thrive while managing their caring responsibilities.

The NHS doesn't create a carer friendly workplace where supporting carers is embedded in the organisation. Look at the behaviour of managers like Siobhan, look at the culture, supporting carers is missing.

NHS England may be committed to embedding a kind approach to carers but that doesn't mean it will happen. Everything depends on who manages you and their personal approach to supporting staff who are carers.

There is a massive level of unmet need in our hospitals and communities, over the years this unmet need has increased and created pressure elsewhere in the system and that, has landed with unpaid carers and families. They spend their time juggling with life and caring for their loved ones.

Gaining my qualifications took me to better paid jobs, in reality, my education came from being present, listening and observing. Extending my knowledge came from witnessing and providing good care to patients.

My last comment on quality, don't take a time approach to change, be bold, push it, test it out, don't be afraid.

Have I been too hard on the staff and hospitals I have written about, I hope not. Choosing between my memories has been hard and yes some of it is boring but jobs are eventually. I hope I have been balanced in this book and that you understand they are my memories. Don't be afraid to complain when you or your family visit or stay in a hospital that's how they learn.

The easy thing was typing the book. Formatting the pages and adding a line or two has taken me so long because every time I changed a word or sentence the whole book moved, it's been a nightmare. I know some of you will understand this. Sorry for any errors, I did my best.

WORDS AND PHRASES

Every day on wards and in offices a common saying will be heard by anyone in the area. I have attached these words to the jobs I performed for the NHS and the CQC.

Nursing Auxiliary / Nursing Support Worker (Band 2 and Band 3)

"Just a minute". "Tea and Toast"? "I won't be long". "Can you hang on"? "Pop a gown on". "Pop on the bed". "Shuffle back until you can feel the chair on your legs". "Can I have a hand"? "Just popping to theatre". "Sorry you had to wait". "Is anyone free"?

Doctors Associate (Band 4) Lead Doctors Associate (Band 5)

"A sharp scratch". "Is it possible to add a patient to the list"? "How high be specific"? "Can you do this test urgently"? "Bleep xxxx". "Are the results ready"? "How long is long"? "When is the test being done"? "Can I have the old X-Rays"? "Sorry you had to wait"

"What does that say"? "It's not a CVA this isn't an accident". "You cannot smell alcohol it's a colourless odourless liquid". "A-copier/copia does not mean the patient cannot cope, it means unable to copy".

ABC Manager
Out Patient Access Manager (Band 6)

"Is the theatre list full"? "Can you add another patient"? "Do we have any theatre cancellations we can use"? "How far ahead is the clinic fully booked"? "Can you produce a list of long waiters"? "More lists have been initiated for the weekend". "Send the letters by taxi". "Sorry you had to wait". "What is your hospital number"? "How many reviews have you to do"? "What did they do"? Can you produce? Collate the information?

Listening into Action (LIA) Associate (Band 6) LIA Lead (Band 7)

"What's LIA"? – "Bottom-up support". "How can we help you achieve your goals"? "Let's engage with your staff". "What is your priority/idea"? "Go on, we will support you all the way". "You can make a difference". "Look, what you have achieved". "Well done". "What a fantastic team". "Has the food been ordered"? "How many are attending"?

CQC Special Advisor
(Around £1,000 plus expenses per inspection)

"Safe – Effective – Caring – Responsive – Well Led". "Hello my name is". "We have been preparing for weeks and spent so much money". "Can I see the evidence"?

"What did you find"? "Patients' mentioned". "How do know your patients are protected, safe and cared for"? "What do you think about leadership in this area"? "What informs you you're meeting the needs of your patients"? "Governance – staff and patient involvement".

Quality Improvement Lead (Band 7, 8a and 8b)

"What's QI"? – "Top-down support". "The wards are to focus on (next new thing)". "We're attending a conference". "We're preparing for the CQC". "We need to",". "We are on training". "Wowing the wards" (clearing out all the crap that has been there for years). "DTOC" (delayed transfer of care) lots of acronyms. "We are doing literature searches this week". "I'm going to a meeting". "We are collecting data; can you complete"? "She's working from home". "Resilience", "resilience". "I will ask if we can allocate time to help your area".

THE WITNESS

Working in any large organisation you witness many situations some absolutely amazing, others that give you the shivers and countless that disappoint you. I witnessed numerous situations and conversations that sadden me too. I believe the amazing moments and situations definitely outweigh the others for me.

The best moments watching patients recover from surgery after witnessing them in pain or the surgery that changed their lives for the better. Of course, the laughter, so many nice moments of giggling and laughing with patients. The sad things I witnessed affected patients for example when they were given a terrible diagnosis and watching their family try to absorb such life distressing news. I was always disappointed when I observed urine bottles on patients' tables next to food trays. Another disappointment was seeing staff walk past patients that were not covered with blankets exposing their private parts to everyone on the ward or while they were being pushed down the corridor.

Some of the unacceptable situations I witnessed include watching a ward clerk run a ward because the manager was ineffective.

Overhearing directors use derogatory terms when discussing a workforce, that was so disappointing.

339

So many times, being made aware that a manager had promoted or given a job to a family member or increased the pay of a team member without going through the process of application and interview. These were always done at the whim of the manager because they needed them in that moment.

I applied and was interviewed for an assistant directorate manager position at one hospital only to discover the post had been temporarily pulled, as the directorate manager and his secretary were suspended for looking at porn on the hospital computer. Another interview I recall running rings around the interviewers because they had little experience of working in the NHS. So disappointing.

Seeing many staff devote their life's work to the NHS to a so-called caring organisation only to witness it betray them time and again that was disappointing to watch and very sad.

Observing fabulous teamwork has been one of the highlights of my career. I met amazing teams working on wards looking after patients and their colleagues. I watched numerous remarkable administration teams throughout all parts of the hospitals, all making huge contributions to provide a positive experience for our patients.

Finally, my favourite teams, the DAs and the junior doctors, dedicated, hardworking and generous.

The NHS has provided me with amazing training and educational support plus some good friends, many fabulous colleagues and a not too shabby career and for that I'm grateful.

While writing this book I recalled many lovely people and times. I seem to talk about favourites a lot, well it's true I realised many people I worked with were special to me. Nurses, doctors, admin staff and ward clerks, if I mentioned you, I loved our interaction and working with you.

LIFE IN THE NHS

ACKNOWLEDGEMENTS

Thanks to colleagues, patients and families, for making such a difference to my working life. Some of my memories are full of laughter others hard work and some heart ache. I applaud the bravery and honesty of patients and staff I met. Big hug to anyone that made me laugh and to all at the heart of my journey. I'm acknowledging my wonderful husband Vin for his support and listening to my stories. Thanks to my children and friends for getting me out of the negative thoughts, the bad moods and angry moments I've had in life. Their support prevented me from going too far or becoming overly jaded. Thanks to those that helped me through and kept me laughing: Don't forget I remember weird things

Cheers to: -

Friends and former colleagues who were aware of my intention, post-retirement to type what I remember about life in a rundown hospital North of Manchester.

The manager on Gynaecology who hung her washing to dry in the offices rather than at home.

Chris Pollard, the girl with Tina Turner legs, who always thought I was winging it. My bed making buddy.

Shanti Boodhai for amazing support during bad times, I do hope your retirement wish came true – that you eat whatever and whenever you want.

Amanda Brazendale sitting on the desk swinging your legs chatting away with one of the surgeons, you looked like father and daughter you got on so well, but I remember you as cocky and full of confidence, I liked that. I remember our conversations during your difficult times.

Katy the cheeky red-haired staff nurse I met on B1, I only had to look at you and I would smile you were full of banter and had a funny comment or remark to say about most topics. Love you and your wonderful smile.

Heather Wardle calm and unassuming, I remember you learning to drive.

Tracy, you used to twiddle a chunk of hair at the back of your head, your comforter. A sister cut it off, you went mad. Shanti was that you?

I remember the sister who used the term "alright cock" when addressing patients and staff, she was very hands on and like a whirling dervish.

Margaret the auxiliary from B2 who ate bacon and beans a lot. Everyone dieted on a regular basis and Julie comes to mind for saying that eating two Weetabix every day kept her slim.

Then there was Angie Phillips, soft skin, my sauna partner who occasionally had her own way of doing things like sprinkling antibiotic powder on wounds when doing dressings.

Pat who assessed me during my NVQs, my mentor, thanks for always being positive.

Ladies, I can still see your faces and I'm sorry if I haven't mentioned you by name. A big thank you, I loved working with you all, nurses from that time are still working on the surgical wards in 2024, still making a difference to those patients.

Doctors at all levels. A huge thank you for the education the laughter and the care you gave to me and those round me. I adored those weird and funny nights out and the unusual conversations. God you were all so bloody nice.

Jackie Eaton and Pat Phillips good friends and generous people. See you in the Same Yet in Prestwich.

ABC / Booking and Scheduling:

Special thanks to: Nicola, Claire, Dawn, Jerish, Maxine, Julie, Catherine, Michelle, Joanne, Lesley and Zoe. Sorry too many to mention. Appreciations to the supervisors who ran the department, Tracy who should have managed the place fantastic knowledge. Nicola and Alan for providing me with great support. Tariq, even though we had our confrontations I couldn't have managed without your skills and knowledge and finally Ann quietly getting through the day.

LiA: Special thanks to:

Julie Owen for allowing me to be part of a wonderful team, for your generosity and friendship. Lynn Rigby a friend, amazing support and a great lunch buddy.
Staff in the education department.
Medical illustration teams for innovative support.
The best Chef FGH for your Cheese and Onion pie every other Wednesday. Famous

Photographic Acknowledgements: Special thanks to those in the pictures, good times with caring people. The Manchester Evening News article and photo.

POEM "WHO CARES?"

Eyes that speak volumes and a silent tongue,
no verbal outlet to convey what's wrong.
Who cares about this man's affair's, the ailing
woman's needs, or how she succeeds?
In steps the carer, but they're not just that,
they are a shopper, a cook, they may feed the cat
A joker, a psychologist on lend, a medicine
dispenser, an ear to bend.
Trained, uniformed and trusted to care, with gloves
on hand, an ally to interpersonal flair.
Promoting independence building confidence too,
with a dignified manner tenets that adorn the
sectors banner.
Thanks to the carers and their oft unheralded toil,
people that need them don't go to spoil
Those eyes that spoke volumes are now
understood, the tongue that was silent is unmuted
for good

By Joe Bailey A carer

Final Message

Love the NHS
One day there will be no denial.
Thank you for giving up your precious time
to read my blathering's.

References

https://www.manchester.gov.uk/directory_record/212
444/crumpsall_workhouse/category/1371/workhouse
https://en.wikipedia.org/wiki/North_Manchester_Gen
eral_Hospital
http://www.listeningintoaction.co.uk/LiA-info/
England J 2020 (NHS Dirty Secrets) Published
by Amazon Italia Logistica A R.L. Torrazza
Piemonte (TO) Italy
https://www.cqc.org.uk/news/releases/cqc-finds-
pennine-acute-hospitals-nhs-trust-be-inadequate
https://uk.linkedin.com/in/ian-railton-60b7b550

Printed in Great Britain
by Amazon